St. Louis Community College

Forest Park
Florissant Valley
Meramec

Instructional Resources
St. Louis, Missouri

MEA CULPA

A SOCIOLOGY OF

APOLOGY AND

RECONCILIATION

Mea Culpa

A SOCIOLOGY OF APOLOGY

AND RECONCILIATION

Nicholas Tavuchis

STANFORD UNIVERSITY PRESS

STANFORD, CALIFORNIA

1991

Stanford University Press
Stanford, California
© 1991 by the Board of Trustees of the
Leland Stanford Junior University
Printed in the United States of America

CIP data appear at the end of the book

To Bess

Preface

In this work I have tried to shed light on a dimension of social life that is at once commonplace and familiar, and a potentially important cultural resource for tempering antagonisms and resolving conflicts. Specifically, I am concerned with situations in which we (individually or collectively) do or say something that violates a moral imperative, harms someone, and endangers our social standing but is not necessarily subject to formal or legal sanctions. In addition, there are no extenuating circumstances or attempts to conceal, deny, or justify what has been done. Hence, we are accountable for violating a social norm.

Assuming that we are not indifferent to the negative consequences of our conduct, one way we can try to rehabilitate ourselves and restore social harmony is to plead *mea culpa* (through my fault) and apologize to the wronged party. In so doing, we acknowledge the fact of wrongdoing, accept ultimate responsibility, express sincere sorrow and regret, and promise not to repeat the offense. But there is much more to it than this. As I shall try and show, the production of a satisfactory apology is a delicate and precarious transaction. It cannot, for example, be reduced to the mere repudiation of one's untoward words or deeds, because this is manifestly impossible, alien to the spirit of contrition, and self-defeating. To put it another way, we cannot undo what we have done and admitted doing, on the one hand, or forgive what is explainable, on the other. Instead, I argue that the singular achievement of apologetic discourse paradoxically resides in its capacity to effectively eradicate the consequences of the offense by evoking the unpredictable faculty of forgiveness. As a secular ritual of expiation whose essential medium is speech, apology is thus deeply implicated in the central human predicaments of transgression and reconciliation.

Although my theoretical approach is grounded in sociology, I have also drawn upon the insights and findings of philology, sociolinguistics, social psychology, anthropology, philosophy, law, and religion in trying to develop a coherent formulation of apology and its role primarily, but not exclusively, in contemporary Western society. (Needless to say, a more comprehensive account of this phenomenon—but one beyond the purpose or scope of this essay—would entail its investigation in different cultural contexts and historical settings. This remains to be done, as indicated by the qualifying subtitle of this work.) My descriptive materials are equally eclectic and, apart from the few commentaries on apology available in the sociological and allied literatures, include comic strips, aphorisms, ethnographies, fiction, etiquette manuals, and journalistic sources.

The major questions I have tried to address in this effort are the following: What is apology? What are its functions and its essential and variable elements? How do apologies differ from accounts, excuses, disclaimers, and justifications? What forms does apology take in our own culture and in other cultures such as Japan? How is apologetic discourse taught and learned? What are the subjective or experiential dynamics of apology? What is the relation of apology to forgiveness?

My scholarly debts and intellectual bloodlines, for those interested in such matters, are acknowledged in my citations. But there are other gratitudes that should be expressed here. A leave fellowship from the Social Sciences and Humanities Research Council of Canada was instrumental in giving me the time to begin this project. For this I am grateful.

During the course of this study, a number of individuals have helped me clarify my thinking and encouraged me in other ways. It is with great pleasure, therefore, that I record my debts of appreciation to John Condry, Raymond F. Currie, Lawrence F. Douglas, Gail Geller, Rose K. Goldsen, Chauncey Hare, Rodney M. Kueneman, Robert K. Merton, Raymond A. Morrow, Hubert J. O'Gorman, Gibb S. Pritchard, Edward T. Pryor, George Psathas, G. N. Ramu, Robert J. Smith, Stephanos C. Tavuchis, Wayne E. Thompson, Mikhail Vitkin, and Kurt H. Wolff.

Special thanks are owed to Cynthia F. Epstein and William J. Goode for their wise counsel and support over the years.

I would also like to express my gratitude to Grant Barnes and his able staff at Stanford University Press for their congeniality and excellent editorial advice.

Penultimately, no words can possibly convey the depths of my affection and esteem for Charles D. Axelrod and Johann W. Mohr. Both were at my side every step of the way and remain the best of intellectual companions and dearest of friends.

Finally, the dedication, proffered with love, speaks for itself.

N.T.

Contents

MEA CULPA

A SOCIOLOGY OF

APOLOGY AND

RECONCILIATION

I. *The Social Import of Apology*

I trace my interest in apology to a bitter argument I had many years ago with someone close and dear to me. The precise details have faded from memory, but I can still recall feeling hurt, wronged, and angered by the accusations of misconduct and insensitivity. Moreover, the charges seemed to go beyond my alleged transgression. They not only reflected (in my eyes) a harsh judgment of my character but also struck at the very core of our relationship. As our disagreement grew more heated, I finally said that nothing less than a full and sincere apology would clear the air and set things right between us. At the time, I had only a vague notion of what might constitute a "full and sincere apology," and it really didn't matter in light of my agitated emotional state. The day after this painful encounter, I received a short letter expressing sorrow and asking for my forgiveness. At our next meeting, the apology was repeated orally and after I accepted it, we both agreed to forget the matter.

Sometime later, I recalled this poignant incident when something I had said (or done) jeopardized a cherished friendship and moved me to apologize in order to redeem myself. The reminder of this incident, and of other similar incidents, somehow stirred my curiosity about the nature of apology. Was it possible that this mundane, yet mysteriously potent, symbolic act had something important to tell us about social life? What circumstances evoke a seemingly deep-rooted need to cleanse and heal social rifts by means of apology rather than excuses, defenses, justifications, or legal measures? In other words, was there something about apologies that set them apart from other responses to the inevitable grievances generated in social intercourse?

I began to keep track of apologies within my limited social domain and was struck by the frequency with which they played a central role in various situations. Needless to say, these observations were neither systematic nor theoretically guided but what I thought anyone could see with the naked eye. What they revealed was that apologies abound and figure prominently in often invisible and unnoticed normative patterns that shape our moral expectations and sensibilities. These range from trivial, but not thereby unimportant, apologies offered to maintain some modicum of social equilibrium such as the hurried "sorry" evoked by minor incivilities or mishaps to more serious breaches. When queried, virtually every one of us can recall some painful exchange involving an apology in our relations with kin, spouses, lovers, friends, neighbors, co-workers, superiors, subordinates, and strangers. We, in turn, are equally likely to desire (or demand) apologies from others, no matter how close or distant, for real or imagined transgressions. This casual survey indicated that not only is an enormous amount of social energy expended on maintaining acceptable levels of order and predictability but that calls for apology were conspicuous in such ongoing moral projects. It also revealed that the appeal or resort to apology as a way of dealing with normative breaches is not limited to those directly involved. On the contrary, we regularly exhort others to apologize (and to forgive), as when, for example, children and other social novices are instructed in the delicate arts of pacification and conciliation. (I shall have more to say about this particular context later.)

In addition to attending more closely to my immediate surroundings, I began to monitor the ephemeral and selected events reported by newspapers and other mass media. Again, I was impressed by the number of accounts in which apologies were central and considered worthy of public notice. Such items confirmed my hunch about their frequency and further showed that apologies were common to all levels and sectors of society. For example, these encounters included a disgraced President of the United States eliciting the outrage of citizens and media for refusing to at least apologize for his misdeeds; a customer asking the manager of a supermarket for an apology after finding a foreign object in a pork chop; criminals apologizing to their victims; minority groups demanding apologies from private and public organizations for alleged injustices and humiliations; apologies between nations, and many more.

If there was any discernible theme in these often commonplace and sometimes dramatic stories, it appeared to revolve about the violation of an unstated, but consequential, moral rule whose binding force had relatively little to do with legal remedies or considerations. Although the threat of judicial action might be invoked at some point, the paramount concern of the wronged party was the receipt of an apology. Minimally, this entailed acknowledgment of the legitimacy of the violated rule, admission of fault and responsibility for its violation, and the expression of genuine regret and remorse for the harm done. These commonalities were evident whether the principals in question were individuals or collectivities of various kinds.

I continued to collect and file instances of apology as well as to share my inchoate ideas about their meaning with amused, if sympathetic, colleagues, students, and friends. These conversations were, in fact, frustrating because I remained puzzled as to the significance of apologies, how they worked, and their wider social import. An extensive search of diverse sources, including anthropology, psychology, philosophy, law, diplomacy, etiquette manuals, and literature, for examples and commentaries was not, for the most part, fruitful. There are, of course, numerous theological works on the related but, for my purposes, distinct phenomenon of religious confession. As it turned out, journalistic accounts provided most of the concrete descriptions I have used throughout this essay. Finally, although sociology (my own discipline) and linguistics furnished some tantalizing leads, they had little to offer in the way of a sustained analysis of the essentials, forms, and functions of apology.[1]

At first glance, apologies seem so simple and straightforward.

Something happens; something is said or done that is interpreted and judged offensive, improper, or harmful. An apology is called for, someone apologizes, the apology (let us assume) is accepted, the offender is forgiven, and life goes on *as if* nothing had happened. Although some tension may remain—we are, after all, creatures endowed with the faculty of memory—for all practical purposes, the social slate is wiped clean. So commonplace, frequent, widespread, taken for granted, and yet so mysterious, is this occurrence.

This stark paradigm—the complexities it generates will become evident as we proceed—immediately raises a number of questions. Can it be that in its apparent simplicity an apology conceals a revelatory potential for informing us about deeper truths and normative principles of social life? Or are apologies little more than anachronistic and hollow gestures, curious survivals, or ironic clichés in a culture tediously portrayed as morally incoherent, fragmented, and "narcissistic"? And what place can apologies have in a society permeated with litigiousness and increasingly subject to legal and administrative rules? Moreover, as many concerned observers have suggested, has not the guiding precept of Rabelais' Abbey of Thélème, *Fay ce que vouldras* (Do what you will), come to serve as the most apt motto of our time? Finally, is it not clear that virtually any questionable private or public actions, assuming any such remain or are capable of offending, can be casually relegated to the linguistic and moral limbos of "variant lifestyles," "self-actualization," and "situational ethics"? Now if such commentaries and judgments on what we have come to, and have become, are anywhere near the mark, they pose a fundamental question: *what can possibly call for an apology?* Let us consider some of the implications of such arguments.

It is difficult to state with any certainty whether nowadays we show a lesser propensity to apologize than in past times or recognize fewer occasions that specifically call for apologies. Knowledge of such evanescent and often private social facts is not easy to come by or amenable to enumeration. Although some might assert that the call itself—a small but haunting moral voice—has been drowned out and weakened in its capacity to move us because of the din of competing expectations or the general decline of civility, my own impressions, probings, and experience indicate, as suggested earlier, that this singular human faculty is far from being moribund or inconsequential. In fact, as we shall see, there is substantial evidence of a strong and abiding commitment to a general norm of apology, that is, the obligation to apologize for social infractions as opposed to some other course of action, and its applications in particular situations. Moreover, as I shall try and show, apologies constitute strategic instances that illuminate complex social processes and the intricacies of moral commitments. At the same time, the practical ramifications of apology and forgiveness will be considered. As impersonal and legal systems of social control proliferate in our own culture and in other cultures, apologies may loom even larger than they have in the past as voluntary and humane means for reconciling personal and collective differences.[2]

The Paradox and Power of Apology

Apart from their frequency in a variety of settings, which obviously do not distinguish apologies from other acts concerned with social pacification, there was something else about them that aroused my curiosity and wonder. I was, and continue to be, struck by certain paradoxical and talismanic qualities of this human faculty. Specifically, if the major task of apology is to resolve conflicts and somehow restore an antecedent moral order by expunging or eradicating the harmful effects of past actions, then at one level of reality this is manifestly impossible and doomed to fail. Why is this so? Very simply, because an apology, no matter how sincere or effective, does not and cannot *undo* what has been done. And yet, in a mysterious way and according to its own logic, this is precisely what it manages to do. In this regard, Disraeli astutely and pointedly reminds us that "apologies only account for that which they do not alter." While this observation accurately addresses one side of the apparent contradiction we have posed, our interest is drawn to the other. What can this emphasis mean or imply in light of the call for an apology in the first place? To put it another way, is it true that an apology is only (or merely) a discursive gesture that responds to its calling by telling us to pass over and accept what happened? If so, why even bother with an apology after causing distress and harm to another? On the other hand, why doesn't the injured party simply forgive (or suffer) and forget without going through the motions of calling for an apology? But what happens then to the current and future meaning of the broken rule with respect to the moral grounds of the relationship and the possibility that something more than the immediate or personal interests of the offended may be at stake?[3]

Disraeli's aphorism unquestionably tells us something of cardinal importance about apology—that it does *not* alter. At the same time, the use of the restrictive qualifier "only" diverts attention from the transfigurative capacity of this social act, a mysterious quality that will reveal itself throughout this work. The assertion, to reiterate, is that an apology does *one* thing only: it recalls ("accounts for") that which neither the offender nor the offended can change, a fait accompli. Such a formulation thus assumes a cynical, realistic, arrogant, indifferent, or naive perpetrator—the wrongdoer's motives or character are not critical—but, in its own way, raises the deeper question of what moves the offender to apologize, that is, the perceived necessity of an account. Surely it is reasonable to suppose that the victim is also aware that the apology cannot alter. Assuming that we are dealing with a relatively serious violation, and excluding the possibility of cruel irony or the gratuitous addition of insult to injury, can we rest assured that this is the *only* thing an apology can achieve? Does it not also entail some pang of sorrow and regret and acknowledge the moral legitimacy of what was presumed to be mutually binding? In a circuitous fashion, then, Disraeli's insight provides us with an occasion for reflecting upon the almost miraculous qualities of a satisfying apology. And this consists, in part, of forgiveness and reconciliation, which effectively transmute trespasses and prevent them from becoming permanent obstructions to social relations despite the inexorable fact of betrayal.[4]

The American satirist Ambrose Bierce, another master of the sardonic maxim, also had something of interest to say about apology that will concern us. Whereas Disraeli laconically marks the hollow potential of apologetic speech by stressing current inequities stemming from past misdeeds, Bierce looks forward and focuses on its self-serving potential. To apologize, therefore, is "to lay the foundation for a future offense."[5] If we now juxtapose the two—"Apologies only account for that which they do not alter and lay the foundation for future offenses"—we come up with a version of apology that few of us would fail to recognize, but also one that would seem to exclude the regenerative potential of apology and its capacity to transform unbearable realities through speech. For what Bierce and Disraeli oblige us to consider in their penetrating brevity are impoverished and degenerate possibilities. This judgment, I hasten to add, is neither homiletic nor sentimental. There is no doubt whatsoever that individuals and groups routinely employ the language of apology in self-interested and exploitive ways: this is not at issue or contestable. But what is moot is whether such forms of speech can qualify as anything other than caricatures of the potentially transcendent role of apology in human affairs. At the same time, to dismiss the partial truths revealed in these compacted formulations, no less be persuaded by their pithy elegance, would deprive us of an invaluable analytical insight at this preliminary stage of our inquiry. Apart from providing us with exemplars of incomplete or spurious apologetic discourse by focusing on one contingency, namely, the devious author of inauthentic speech, they serve to remind us of the essential relational character of apology. As I shall try and demonstrate, apology speaks to something larger than any particular offense and works its magic by a kind of speech that cannot be contained or understood merely in terms of expediency or the desire to achieve reconciliation.

Apology and Membership

This broader theme, I submit, is concerned with the fundamental sociological question of the grounds for membership in a designated moral community. Such membership claims, as many others have pointed out, are neither self-evident nor self-validating. They must be acknowledged and certified by others who, in addition to various other markers, use visible social compliance (or its absence) as a sign of moral commitment. Thus the validity and stability of our relationships and group affiliations are predicated upon our knowledge, acceptance, and conformity to specific and general norms.

In these admittedly general terms, then, apology expresses itself as the exigency of a painful re-membering, literally of being mindful again, of what we were and had as members and, at the same time, what we have jeopardized or lost by virtue of our offensive speech or action. And it is only by *personally* acknowledging ultimate responsibility, expressing genuine sorrow and regret, and pledging henceforth (implicitly or explicitly) to abide by the rules, that the offender simultaneously recalls and is re-called to that which binds. As shared mementos, apologies require much more than admission or confession of the unadorned facts of wrongdoing or deviance. They constitute—in their most responsible, authentic, and, hence, vulnerable expression—a form of self-punishment that cuts deeply because we are obliged to retell, relive, and seek forgiveness for sorrowful events that have rendered our claims to membership in a moral community suspect or defeasible. So it is that the call for an apology always demands and promises more than it seems to. As anyone who has ever apologized in these circumstances well knows, the act is always arduous and painful, whether done voluntarily or at the urging of others. And yet, when this secular rite of expiation is punctiliously performed, and the remorseful admission of wrongdoing is converted into a gift that is accepted and reciprocated by forgiveness, our world is transformed in a way that can only be described as miraculous. All the more so because the gesture itself reiterates the reality of the offense while superseding it.

Illustrative documentation for the interpretation of apology I have been trying to fashion thus far may be adduced in the treatment of the topic in a widely syndicated North American comic strip, "Gil Thorp," whose setting is a high school in a small city. The story line of the first episode concerns Bobby Loft, an outstanding athlete, who has been having academic and personal difficulties with his teachers and peers.[6] He has been tormenting one of his teachers, a young widow, unaware that his widower father has fallen in love with her. Coach Thorp and others have been trying to straighten the boy out with little success. In addition to isolating him from other pupils, Loft's malicious behavior has jeopardized his relationship with a girl to whom he is attracted. In previous strips he apologized to the girl for his actions and promised to change his ways. The teacher (Mrs. Tyson) is reluctant to tell his father about her problems with the boy, fearing that such a disclosure would harm their budding romance. Loft must do well in his studies to remain on the team. (See pp. 10–11.)

The second episode focuses on a member of the football team, Dean Dalton, who is also taking ballet lessons.[7] Rumors begin circulating that he is a homosexual. In a crucial game, Alfie (one of his teammates) tells the opposing players that Dalton is indeed homosexual and, as a consequence, the latter is severely injured. When Thorp learns of all this, he benches Alfie and, as a result, the game is lost. The other coaches urge Thorp to find out if Dalton is homosexual (he is not), but he refuses on the grounds that this is a private matter and not relevant to his team membership or performance. Coach Thorp resolves the matter by having Alfie apologize to Dalton publicly. (See p. 11.)

Although these examples may appear trivial and contrived, they dramatically, concisely, and cogently reveal certain underlying assumptions concerning apology. To wit: they are difficult and potentially humiliating; there is a tendency to resist apologizing that must be overcome; apologies call attention to what we may *be* as well as what we have done; failure to apologize may endanger valued social ties; some forms of transgression can be remedied only by apology; apology has the power to rehabilitate the individual and restore social harmony. It should also be noted that both the artistic and commercial success of this and other kinds of popular cultural productions, for example, musical lyrics, derive from their ability to express and shape recognizable, shared, and unquestioned premises and meanings. And finally, we should not underestimate the media's didactic function. As they depict, they also remind and instruct their audiences.

All these preliminary, unfocused, and often perplexing efforts to understand the social import of apology inevitably led to the con-

sideration of a number of related and, at first, equally abstract questions. For example, in addition to the problematics of membership, a formulation of what apologies express and the contexts in which they appear requires that we reexamine some supposedly secure assumptions about normative systems, forms of social control, and different reactions to transgressions. Since these matters will be taken up in greater detail later, I shall do little more here than briefly anticipate some of the pertinent theoretical points and arguments.

Apologies and Social Order

Let us begin with the obvious. Every social order depends, by definition, on some measure of commitment to norms dealing with standards of behavior and institutional arrangements, many of which are tacit, inarticulate, or obscured by habit or design. For the most part, members are socialized (some more effectively than others) to treat customary or arbitrarily imposed rules as self-evident to the extent that they go unnoticed unless the social traffic they unobtrusively regulate is disrupted, blocked, or diverted from conventional cultural arteries.[8]

These sociological truisms suggest that the smoother a particular system of interaction operates, whether it entails the production of an appropriate greeting, marriage, or economic transaction, for example, the more difficult it is to decipher without reference to the unstated cultural premises upon which it is predicated. An important corollary of the relative opacity of stable social configurations and processes is that our understanding of their meanings is likely to be enhanced in the presence of disturbance or deviation. In other words, whatever the source, disruptions of established social procedures generate disparities, asymmetries, contrasts, oppositions, ambiguities, and compensatory reactions that lay bare, if only fleetingly, organizing principles. Thus, in both intimate and impersonal settings, characteristic responses to violations of privileged moral standards and expectations can provide us with critical occasions for delving into covert social agendas that buttress prevailing definitions of order, predictability, and valid membership.[9] For our purposes, apologies can illuminate such matters in at least two ways. First, they are potentially sensitive indicators of members' (and non-members') actual, if unspoken, moral orientations. Second, as symbolic barometers, apologies register tensions and displacements in personal and public belief systems, that is, the contraction and expansion of interdictory motifs—what calls for an apology and what does not—that either precede or follow changes in social behavior and cultural expectations.

Putting aside, for the moment, what members are expected to know at different stages of their moral careers, differential commitment to rules, local definitions of venial and capital offenses, the social units involved, etc., we may provisionally note that apologies have to do with an ineluctable reality of human interaction—the possibility of transgression by word or deed.[10] Because, as suggested earlier, they simultaneously represent (and reenact) consummated infractions and attempts to reclaim membership, they unequivocally enunciate the existence and force of shared assumptions that authorize existing social arrangements and demarcate moral boundaries. That is to say, we not only apologize *to* someone but also *for* something. The analytical focus of the former is on actors, agents, and social relationships; the latter, by contrast, directs attention to rules and meta-rules, that is, rules about rules.[11] Needless to say, both perspectives must be considered in developing a valid account of apology.

Genuine apologies, from all that has been said, may be taken as the symbolic foci of secular remedial rituals that serve to recall and reaffirm allegiance to codes of behavior and belief whose integrity has been tested and challenged by transgression, whether knowingly or unwittingly. An apology thus speaks to an act that cannot be undone but that cannot go unnoticed without compromising the current and future relationship of the parties, the legitimacy of the violated rule, and the wider social web in which the participants are enmeshed. This latter point, the transpersonal implications, will be discussed more thoroughly as our formulation unfolds, but merits at least passing comment here because apologies tend to be associated with interpersonal or intimate bonds that exclude others.

A consummate apology, no matter how personal or private an act, is rarely the sole concern of the principals. It is not easily contained because it inevitably touches upon the lives and convictions of interested others while raising both practical and moral questions that transcend the particular situation that prompted it. In this sense, it is quintessentially social, that is, a *relational* symbolic gesture occurring in a complex interpersonal field, with enormous reverberatory potential that encapsulates, recapitulates, and pays homage to a moral order rendered problematic by the very act that calls it forth. As prototypes of relatively spontaneous, overt, and swift responses to transgressions, apologies accomplish much and do so economically. They commemorate and reproduce ethical axioms while calling attention to authorized definitions of reality, that is, objective, but not necessarily specified, limits and moral boundaries for individuals and groups.

These introductory remarks and conjectures suggest that an investigation of apology is not only worthwhile in its own right but affords a unique and fruitful perspective for readdressing the basic sociological questions of membership, deviance, and conformity. Let us now begin our inquiry by attempting to clarify the meanings, nature, and functions of apology with greater specification, using etymology as our point of departure.

2. Meanings, Nature, and Functions of Apology

The Etymology of Apology

Austin, among others, has observed that "our common stock of words embodies all the distinctions men have found worth drawing and the connexions they have found worth marking in the lifetimes of many generations: these surely are likely to be more numerous, more sound, since they have stood up to the long test of the survival of the fittest, and more subtle, at least in all ordinary and reasonably practical matters, than any that you or I are likely to think up in our arm-chairs of an afternoon—the most favoured alternative method."[1]

I shall begin this part of our inquiry by taking Austin's proposal seriously and pose the following questions: what is the provenance of the word *apology* and what, if anything, can a critical interrogation of its pedigree tell us about its contemporary usages and kindred concepts?

Eric Partridge traces the term to its Greek root, *apologos*, a story, from which *apologia*, an oral or written defense, became apology.[2] *The Oxford English Dictionary* (*OED* henceforth) omits any reference to *apologos* as a story and begins from the Greek *apoloyia* (*apo*, away, off; *loyia*, speaking), which is defined as a defense or speech in defense.[3] The first three meanings with the approximate date of first documented usage are as follows:

1. The pleading off from a charge or imputation, whether expressed, implied, or only conceived as possible; a defence of a person or vindication of an institution, etc., from accusation or aspersion. (1533)
2. Less formally: Justification, explanation or excuse of an incident or course of action. (1583)
3. An explanation to a person affected by one's action that no offence was intended, coupled with the expression of regret for any that may have been given; or a frank acknowledgement of the offence with an expression of regret for it, by way of reparation. (1594)

Thus what originally meant a defense or vindication of charges by others came to refer informally to an account in the sense of a justification, explanation, excuse, and later an account of an offense that was unintended. Of interest to us here is the gradual evolution whereby the expression of regret itself serves as reparation without requiring additional actions on the part of the transgressor.

The verb form *apologize* came into use in 1597 according to the *OED*:

To speak in, or serve as, justification, explanation, or palliation of a fault, failure, or anything that may cause dissatisfaction; to offer defensive arguments; to make excuses.

Also in modern usage; To acknowledge and express regret for a fault without defence, by way of reparation to the feelings of the person affected.

Once again, the first given meaning does not distinguish apologies from justifications, excuses, explanations, etc., although what is considered "modern" usage clearly excludes these connotations by the qualifier "without defence." This meaning reiterates that the apology *itself*, that is, the acknowledgment and expression of regret for the fault, constitutes restitution. There is no mention of a promise not to repeat the offense, even though this would not be an unreasonable inference given one's frank avowal and statement of regret. Throughout, it should be noted, there is no explicit reference to sorrow.

Another source clearly differentiates apologies from justifications, explanations, and excuses while expanding upon what the *OED* cites as modern usage:

1. A written or spoken expression of one's regret, remorse, or sorrow for having insulted, failed, injured, or wronged another.
2. A defense, excuse, or justification in speech or writing, as for a cause or doctrine.[4]

There are a number of other ways in which this definition departs from that of the *OED*. First, we are reminded that failure to do or say something may call for an apology. Second, in keeping with the modern emphasis on literacy, these meanings allow for written as well as oral expressions of apology. Finally, whereas the *OED* speaks only of regret, the primary entry here gives equal place to remorse and sorrow. In both sources, the question of future action remains moot and the definitional perspective is that of the transgressor.

The Affective and Discursive Core of Apology

This brief review reveals an interesting connotative displacement and transformation. In earlier times, an apology referred to a defense, justification, or excuse. Its modern meaning and usage have shifted so that now an apology begins where these former rhetorical and essentially self-serving forms leave off. The implications of this semantic divergence for our purposes are not insignificant. To apologize is to declare voluntarily that one has *no* excuse, defense, justification, or explanation for an action (or inaction) that has "insulted, failed, injured, or wronged another." On the other hand, one who offers an account, for example, an excuse or defense, asks the offended party, in effect, to be reasonable by giving explanations that are intended to (partially or fully) release him or her. So it is that such placatory or evasive attempts, no matter how sincere, always seek to divert attention from the agent of action to conventional categories of causality such as incapacity, accident, ignorance, or coercion. In sharp contrast, one who apologizes seeks forgiveness and redemption for what is unreasonable, unjustified, undeserving, and inequitable.

Something else should be noted in these two contexts. Short of eventuating in a complete rupture of relations, transgressions involve the risks of retaliation and the progressive escalation of conflict. Both accounts and apologies strive to counter these tendencies by settling matters, but in quite different ways. On the one hand, the urgency of an account resides in the energy expended in extenuation. The earnestness of an apology, on the other hand, is marked by scrupulous self-exposure to justifiable retribution while pleading for unconditional remission.[5]

Neither of our sources, moreover, alludes to the root *apologos* (story), even though the other meanings given carry this connotation. And this leads us to consider further the distinctive perspectives of apologies and accounts. An apology is a special kind of enacted story whose remedial potential, unlike that of an account, stems from the acceptance by the aggrieved party of an admission of iniquity and defenselessness. It is thus about a fall from social grace related to someone—*the only one*—who has the power to restore the offender to that state. And what is that condition if not a micro-metaphor for secure membership, connectedness, and identity? Needless to say, explanations, excuses, etc., are also stories whose truth value or sincerity may be questioned, accepted, or denied. But they differ from apologies precisely because the narrator invokes *something* (or *someone*) to deny or to mitigate responsibility for an offense that undermines that which unites and binds.

The issue of verisimilitude is much more subtle when we apologize than when we try to convince the other through reason(s) because we stand unarmed and exposed, relying, in a manner of speaking, on our moral nakedness to set things right. Paradoxically, by assuming such a vulnerable stance, and only by so doing, we now unobtrusively shift the burdens of belief and acceptance to the injured party. That such a story and, more important, its telling do not depend upon a natural or cultural *deus ex machina* to extricate us from our plight at once distinguishes an apology from an account and thus engages the interlocutors in moral discourse of an entirely different order. When we apologize, to reiterate, we stand naked. No excuses, appeals to circumstance, etc., can elicit that which alone can release, eradicate, and renew: forgiveness and, hence, redemption.[6]

There is yet another ground for distinguishing apologies from other attempts to remedy and to restore that is intimately related to what I have been discussing. And here, as throughout, sympathetic skeptics are invited to reflect upon their own experiences in judging the validity of the argument. Specifically, when we resort to excuse, explanation, or justification, we necessarily attempt to distance ourselves from our actions and our unique personal identities. We deny or suspend the imperatives of responsibility and answerability. We appeal, variously, to an impaired self, for example, diminished capacity or external forces (coercion, accident, or even, on occasion, the miraculous) to exonerate our doings and their consequences.[7]

An apology, in contrast, requires *not* detachment but acknowledgment and painful embracement of our deeds, coupled with a declaration of regret. Thus the commonplace phrase, "I am sorry," conveys a simple description of one's own condition—a condition that, if accepted as *authentic*, would then warrant forgiveness by the other.

I stress "authentic" because there is a fine but crucial line between an apology and an account—for example, excuse, disclaimer—despite the fact that the two may appear similar or employ the same form of speech. In its purest expression, an apology clearly announces that "I have no excuses for what I did or did not do or say. I am sorry and regretful. I care. Forgive me." To offer an apology and have it rejected because it is "merely" another account signalizes a moral turning point in a relationship. Similarly, what began as an account may end as an apology in some circumstances. In practice, it makes a difference to us in our roles as suppliants and recipients if we interpret a speech as an apology or an account. In thinking about apology and analyzing concrete instances, we have to attend to the differences that make for *that* difference.

If the heart of apology consists of a genuine display of regret and sorrow as opposed to an appeal to reason(s), it behooves us to examine the meaning and implications of *regret*. As before, let us turn to the dictionary for clues:

1. Feel sorrow for loss of, wish one could have again; be distressed about or sorry for (event, fact), grieve at, repent (action etc.); be sorry *to* say etc. or *that* (esp. in polite refusal of invitation etc.).

2. Sorrow for loss of person or thing; repentance or annoyance concerning this done or not done; (real or politely simulated) vexation or disappointment caused by occurrence or situation.[8]

From this we would conclude that the expression of regret (and hence, sorrow) that is essential to an apology speaks to the offended other(s) of a shared loss resulting from one's unreasonable actions. It refers to something done (or not done), said (or unsaid), that betrays and threatens whatever defines, binds, and is deemed worthy. Reason points outward; apologies direct attention inward. Regret, gently but firmly, reminds us of what we were before we erred, what our place was, where we stood in relation to the other, and what we have lost. And regret is sad about this state because it was me, my actions and conduct, and not those of someone else, or conditions beyond my control, that brought about my estrangement. In other words, it was *my* poverty, *my* breach of trust, that led to the loss. Hence, the offender's regret pleads—and must be careful lest the plea be taken as purely instrumental or manipulative—for the restoration of a prior valued state by asking for what is, perhaps, the ultimate humane gesture: redemption without reason.[9]

But there is more to apology than solipsistic yearning. And to understand what this is requires that we attend to what comes before and what follows, that is, a social context. A proper and successful apology is the middle term in a moral syllogism that commences with a *call* and ends with *forgiveness*. The social processes that generate the sequence cannot be activated until there is a call: the attribution and nomination of an offense that can be negotiated not by an account or appeal to reason(s), but only through the faculty of forgiving. In other words, until the action in question is semantically and symbolically transformed into "apologizable" discourse, it remains subject to other formulations and interpretations. These may or may not be concerned with apology's fundamental tasks of reaccrediting membership and stabilizing precarious relations, but what they share is indifference to or incapacity for forgiveness. Thus, depending upon the relative status, interests, resources, moral assumptions, etc., of the participants (and concerned others), different consequences can follow a transgression. It may be punished, avenged, admonished, excused, ignored, denied, defined as venial, or fall outside the boundary of forgiveness altogether. Moreover, the membership status of the offender may be categorically revoked, conditionally suspended, or remain intact. Whatever else such reactions signify, they herald the absence of a call and raise the question of what kinds of offenses qualify as "apologizable" and, hence, forgivable. Let us examine this issue of apologetic thresholds and transgressional metrics more closely.

If, as suggested earlier, apologies take up where accounts leave off, then what members of a group or culture view as too minor an offense is not likely to call for an apology and its concomitant expressions of regret and sorrow. Thus, where an actor's responsibility and intentionality are deemed to be minimal or the consequences as trivial or accountable, an apology is superfluous.[10] By contrast, too heinous an offense would go beyond the purview of apology and be unforgivable. In this instance, an apology would sound as if it were only making light of the enormity of the transgression and, effectively, offend further. Although many examples of this possibility come to mind—so-called "black" humor is nourished by it— the obituary of one of the most sinister figures in Nazi Germany unequivocally addresses this point in evaluating his memoirs:

Mr. Speer was the only Nazi leader at the Nuremberg war crime trials in 1945–46 to admit his guilt. . . . Most critics praised his candor in writing about the responsibility he bore for Nazi excesses. "My moral failure is not a matter of this item or that," he wrote, in *Inside The Third Reich*. "It resides in my active association with the whole course of events. I had participated in a war which, as we of the intimate circle should never have doubted, was aimed at world domination. What is more, by my abilities and energies, I prolonged the war by many months." Mr. Speer also dealt with the excuse that he knew little or nothing about the death camps. "Whether I knew or did not know, or how much or how little I knew, is totally unimportant when I consider what horrors would have been the natural ones to draw from the little I did know," he wrote. "No apologies are possible."[11]

Speer's complicities so violated human sensibilities that no apology could possibly mollify feelings of violation, outrage, and revulsion in order to call forth the cleansing spirit of forgiveness. And to whom would he have apologized?[12]

The call, to resume our argument, is thus first, the beginning of this moral dialectic. If there is no call, no urgency to remember, no struggle against the natural tendency to forget, then there is no occasion for apology (although there may be occasion for something else), and the process of call, apology, forgiveness, and reconciliation is aborted.[13] Thus, to the extent that we can anticipate, recognize, and name that which only apology can heal *prior* to the call, we are thinking like members. When we respond to the call *after* the offense by apologizing, we are seeking reconfirmation of our credentials as members by publicly recalling their unstated grounds, that is, what we apparently forgot when we transgressed.[14] Just as the precipitating event is transformed into an occasion for apology by virtue of a call, our participation in the ensuing exchange engages us (and our interlocutor[s]) in serious discourse about the moral requisites of interpersonal, group, or collective membership.

If the goal of apology is ultimately forgiveness as a prelude to reunion and reconciliation, then we must convince the other of our worthiness. A difficult and delicate undertaking even when the transgression is minor, it is especially onerous when the violation is deemed to be grave. The task demands close attention to the mode of expression and is complicated further by our defenselessness, shame, and fear of rejection.[15] What is critical, I would argue, is the very act of apology itself rather than the offering of material or symbolic restitution (we cannot undo what has been done, only erase it by seeking forgiveness) or the pledge not to err again (since our actions were unaccountable, this burden would have to be borne by the expression of regret lest it sound hollow or duplicitous).[16] And this suggests that an apology requires our full participation in a particular form of social intercourse.

Apology as a Speech Act

Let us examine the nature of this involvement by noting that an apology is, first and foremost, a speech act.[17] Between individuals, its compelling and poignant qualities derive primarily, but not exclusively, from oral utterance in the immediate presence of another.[18] Initially, there is the "naming" of the offense in the sense of its mutual identification as an apologizable action responsive to a call. This may entail an explicit reference to the breach or an allusion that presumes common knowledge and understanding. For example, "What I (you) did (said) was wrong, harmful, inexcusable, etc." Second, there is the apology itself, whose centerpiece is an expression of sorrow and regret. The final term in this moral equation is the response of the injured party: whether to accept and release by forgiving, to refuse and reject the offender, or to acknowledge the apology while deferring a decision. Although actual sequences and stages may be differentially punctuated with respect to timing, elaboration, articulation, overlap, and so on, this three-phase process encompasses, we would submit, the minimal analytical requirements for the production of an apology.[19]

If there is any merit to this formulation, it follows that an unalloyed apology is not merely another form of impression management, an interactional gambit, or a rhetorical ploy. Something more is at stake in its genesis than the advantages sought in such social maneuvers. To the contrary, an apology is an intricate set of speech acts that is evoked and vivified by actions that challenge the putatively secure achievements of membership in a moral community. An apologizable breach thus constitutes a threat to such an order and its accompanying definitions of reality that calls for the elimination of discrepancy and uncertainty through unmediated confrontation.[20]

It is not surprising, therefore, that although an oral apology may be supplemented by the written word and symbolic tokens of conciliation, the latter, by themselves, are rarely considered to be sufficient or satisfactory. The energizing medium in this decisive auto-da-fé cannot be ignored or underestimated without missing the sociological core of apology. There is, quite simply, nothing as effective and unsettling as having to address in person someone we have wronged, no matter how much a culture stresses writing, print, or electronic communication to the detriment of speech. Our appreciation of this sensory preeminence, especially in connection with such urgent projects as apology and forgiveness, owes much to the sustained and illuminating reflections of Walter J. Ong. For example:

Oral utterance thus encourages a sense of continuity with life, a sense of participation, because it is itself participatory. Writing and print, despite their intrinsic value, have obscured the nature of the word and of thought itself, for they have sequestered the essentially participatory word—fruitfully enough, beyond a doubt—from its natural habitat, sound, and assimilated it to a mark on a surface, where a real word cannot exist at all.[21]

An apology, in this context, speaks regretfully of what one was, had, shared, and lost—without reason. It seeks, through speech, to recover a precious, but tenuous, sense of continuity and to reclaim the unquestioned right to participate as a member.

In another place, the same author reminds us of the centripetal potential inherent in speech and, by implication, its capacity to reunite that which has been sundered by violation:

Thus because of the very nature of sound as such, voice has a kind of primacy in the formation of true communities of men, groups of individuals constituted by shared awareness. A common language is essential for a real community to form. It binds man not only in pairs or families, but, as nothing else does, in large groups, and as a consequence, it has a kind of primacy even between individuals. It would appear that precisely because sound is so interiorizing and thus exploitable by man at depths unknown to less interiorized creatures, it implements socialization or even forces it as nothing else can. True interiority makes it possible to address others; only insofar as a person has interior resources, insofar as he experiences his full self, can he also relate to others, for addressing or relating to them involves him precisely in interiority, too, since they are interiors. Thus addressing others is not quite "facing" them insofar as facing is a visually based concept that calls for turning outward. Communication is more inwardness than outwardness. It is not entirely satisfactory even to say that man is an interior exteriorizing himself. To exteriorize oneself without interiorization is to devote oneself to things, which alone are not satisfying. To address or communicate with other persons is to participate in their inwardness as well as in our own.[22]

The counsel of a best-selling etiquette book, whose publisher states there are "over 2,750,000 copies in use," neatly illustrates some of the distinctive features of apology we have been discussing. It is also instructive, far beyond its intended purpose, insofar as it assumes what any member of a large, if unknown, segment of North American culture would recognize as calling for an apology and accept as a reasonable course of conciliatory conduct. Under the heading

"Letters of Apology," the offending pupil is given the following advice:

A letter of apology should be sincere and rather humble or it probably won't accomplish its mission. Of course, if you owe someone an apology, it's better to make it first face to face, and then reinforce it with a note. If you absolutely cannot face someone to whom you have done an injustice, take pen to paper and humbly ask for forgiveness. For example, a woman who made an ethnic slur in front of a friend who she did not know was of that culture, might write the victim of her remark a letter along the following lines: . . . In saying what I did, I realize I have offended you badly, but myself too, because it was a cruel, stupid, and bigoted remark. I hope someday you will say you forgive me. The episode has taught me a very valuable lesson. I am only sorry that, in learning it, I had to hurt a good friend of mine.[23]

As spectators (or seekers of guidance), we enter into this hypothetical morality play in the beginning of the second act. Something happened—a speech act in the presence of someone identified as a "friend"—that violated a shared, if unstated, rule governing the relationship. However loosely the term "friend" is defined in this context, given the offender's ignorance of the victim's ethnicity, we are presented with an existing relationship that both parties presumably wish to preserve. The event leading to the apology did not become critical in this respect until the offender (in this case) defined it as an apologizable offense and not as something else, for example, an occasion for terminating the friendship or an injustice beyond apology. We have no way of knowing from the example whether the victim shared this definition or not. Consequently, the letter may be seen as an attempt to accomplish two things: to establish the breach as apologizable and to apologize.

We should note here that until there is a mutually understood response to a call (emanating from the offender, offended, or interested third parties), there is no occasion for an apology, and the meaning of the act remains ambiguous or subject to other interpretations. For example, conduct and speech that appear cruel, vicious, and hostile to outsiders may be acceptable badinage between intimates. The victim may choose to ignore depreciatory remarks, no matter how unjust or hurtful, in order to preserve an otherwise cherished bond. The injured party may deny the status of victim by denying the existence of a relationship. For example, "Why should that bigot apologize to me? She says things like that all the time. She isn't, and never has been, a friend of mine." In the same view, and assuming the offender has made apologetic overtures, disparaging actions and remarks may so shatter one's sense of reality that forgiveness is ruled out and any social ties are severed.

To return to the example, we see that the offender does not appeal to extenuating circumstances or impaired capacity but takes full responsibility for her actions. But she has done more than jeopardize the relationship and harm the other; she has diminished herself. Although the brunt of the misdeed is attributed to the speech, only by firmly attaching herself to the "cruel, stupid, and bigoted remark" can the offender avoid converting the apology into an account and license her expression of sorrow as being genuine.

The author of the text stresses the necessity of sincerity and humility for the gesture to accomplish its "mission" or task. It is thus taken for granted that the reader shares her understanding that the quid pro quo in this rhetorical work (and the only way to palliate a sense of guilt and shame, negative self-images and repute, and to save the relationship) is through the forgiveness of the other. Forgiveness, that is, for producing something cruel, stupid, and bigoted as opposed to *being* that kind of person. This requires that a fine balance be struck between accepting full responsibility for one's actions while convincing the other that what occurred does not represent an alternative, but unrevealed, character. It is in these terms that the salience and difficulty of face-to-face confrontation are acknowledged. The written word is acceptable but clearly inferior and, at best, ancillary as indicated by the conditional, "If you absolutely cannot face someone to whom you have done an injustice. . . ." We may further assume from the tone of the suggested paradigm that a positive response from the victim would not end the matter and that the offender would confirm the written intent with oral pleadings. Vanderbilt and others stress the primacy of oral, if not face-to-face, communication for lesser offenses that call for apologies, such as forgetting appointments or missing social engagements. According to these authorities, civility and good form here require a telephone call followed by a written note of apology.

Although this work (and the genre) recognizes that an apology is essentially a speech act that seeks forgiveness, that is, recertification of bona fide membership and unquestioned inclusion within a moral order, and provides the reader with the appropriate discursive tools, it is silent as to how an apology achieves its formidable goal. This is understandable because the primary aim of such social shepherds is to furnish apprehensive readers with pragmatic formulas for coping with standardized and recurrent social breaches. Nevertheless, this fundamental question is addressed, albeit inadvertently, under the subheading "Office manners. Letter of apology for having seriously offended someone." In this didactic example, we are spared any prefatory admonitions about sincerity, humility, etc., and simply provided with a model easily suited to cover a multitude of solecisms between co-workers or, for that matter, any individuals who associate regularly. Although the hypothetical writer of the letter seems tempted to excuse her unstated offense, the moral tenor of the message is apologetic insofar as the desideratum is forgiveness as opposed to understanding on the basis of situational or personal exigencies:

Dear Hank:

   There is no way I can erase the tragic error of my bumbling tongue this morning. I never would consciously offend you in any way, because I respect and treasure your friendship. I hope that along with all the other good qualities you possess, forgiveness is among them. For I need your forgiveness now very much.

Sincerely,
Elizabeth[24]

The efficacy and transformational qualities of an apology can be understood only in relation to its status as a speech act. As noted earlier, an apology cannot annul what has come to pass, yet its sympathetic reception marks an extraordinary and unpredictable social achievement. In the prior example, the offender begins by acknowledging the unalterable nature of her actions. Her goal, therefore, is to transfigure the meaning ascribable to the raw transgression into the idiom of apology, that is, one symbolizing a responsiveness to a call that inaugurates apologetic discourse and is discerned as such by the victim and concerned others. The offensive words cannot be taken back, nor can they be charged to the independent work-ings of an unruly tongue. These possibilities are precluded because the former would effectively deny the experience of the offended party, and the latter, if not taken as a synecdoche, would raise serious questions about the offender's competence and, hence, claims to full membership.[25]

Another commentator on etiquette who is sensitive to the nuances of apology is Judith Martin, author of an internationally syndicated column, "Miss Manners." For example, a correspondent inquires about the correct response when another person apologizes. After disposing of situations in which the offending party was merely being polite or clearly not at fault or malicious, that is, the action was accountable, she provides three variations based upon the severity of the offense and the ways in which the words "Oh, that's quite all right" are expressed:

Acceptance of an apology for an ill-conceived act that offender immediately acknowledges should never have been committed. Guest spills coffee while using filled coffee cup to represent the ocean in a demonstration of naval tac-tics. Host pauses before saying anything, looking at offender with a wooden social smile (lips slightly curved upwards, but no trace of pleasantness else-where in the face). Then says in an expressionless voice, "Oh. That's . . . quite . . . all . . . right."

Acceptance of an apology belatedly offered for a purposely committed major offense, when the offender is not being fully forgiven, but will be allowed to be on probation. Guest makes joke about how bad coffee is, and pours it in the fish bowl, killing valued fish. Host stares guest down with shocked face (eyes blazing, but mouth carefully closed) and pauses so long that the silence is frightening. Then snaps out, "Oh! That's! Quite! All! Right!" as if saying, "I think that's quite enough out of you."

Pseudo-acceptance of an apology for an act for which the offender will never be forgiven. Guest gets into fight with another guest and pours hot coffee over him. Host stands up, posture and face rigid, and waits until he has everyone's attention. Snaps out in sarcastic tones, "Oh, that's quite all right," as if saying, "I can assure you that nothing you can do, ever again, will be of slightest interest to me." Host then whips around, turning back on offender, who will soon notice that he is expected to leave the house immediately and forever.

It is Miss Manners' guess that number three [acceptance of an apology for an ill-conceived act that the offender immediately acknowledges should never have been committed] is the posture you want. In such a case, a combination of remorse and model behavior should, after a suitable period of probation, result in the offense's being expunged from the record.[26]

Martin reiterates these dicta in a brief section on apologies in her book on manners wherein she notes, "People who boast that they 'never apologize, never explain,' or who claim that 'love is never having to say you're sorry' ought to be ashamed of themselves and admit it and ask forgiveness. Now that the duel is illegal, the apology is the only way left to settle many disputes without getting blood on the sofa. A humble speech, a graceful letter, a box of flowers, a duplicate Etruscan vase to replace the one you merrily knocked over to dramatize a story—what fault will these not erase? . . . there are, indeed, unforgivable social sins for which there is no need to apologize because no apology would ever be adequate."[27]

Martin also provides socially fastidious, but errant, readers with an example of a note of apology in response to a serious offense, similar to those found in Vanderbilt:

Dear Aunt Patience:

I shall never forgive myself for that awful scene I caused at your house last night. Daffodil says I should be drummed out of the family and she is quite right. I have no idea who that young lady was, and I don't know what possessed me. I only hope some day to regain your esteem.

Sincerely yours,

Rhino[28]

Although the writer comes perilously close to pleading incapacity ("I don't know what possessed me"), he takes responsibility for his actions, indicates that they were not inevitable, expresses remorse, and accepts the possible sanction of exclusion, although Martin says nothing about a subsequent face-to-face encounter.

In contrast to Vanderbilt and Martin, the latest edition of Emily

Post's venerable *vade mecum*—revised, appropriately enough, by her daughter—contains only two references to letters of apology, which are, in fact, exemplars of accounts:

A note of apology should offer a valid excuse for breaking an engagement. Although you may have telephoned or sent a telegram, a written explanation should follow.

Occasionally an unfortunate accident occurs, which, although it may have been entirely beyond our control, requires that we send another type of note of apology.[29]

Pace Vanderbilt and Martin, apologies (and their formulaic expressions) have a relatively minor role in the world of etiquette, which, following the lead of Post, views itself as sufficiently complete and insulated from the dubious or harmful actions that generate them. More precisely, discourses of this normative genre consist of rules, markers, codes, stagings, anticipatory preparations, sensibilities, resolutions, etc., geared, if followed punctiliously, to avoid situations in which apologies would figure and to minimize the transgressive potential inherent in social intercourse.[30]

Nevertheless, such authorities (and their disciples) also know that these rules and ideals can only be approximated because we can neither control nor foresee everything and because the rules themselves may conflict. Despite the assumption that one who acquires and assiduously consults such a guide is already sensitive to the probability of untoward encounters, some exemplary provisions have to be made for the vagaries of malicious ineptitude, indelicate intrusions, uncertainties of social life, and cultural redefinitions of morals and manners. These rulings, perforce, consist of standardized prescriptions, responses, or strategies (prescriptive, proscriptive, and optional) for coping with socially recognized disruptive contingencies that are uniform, recurrent, and graded. In contrast to the typically bland didactic paradigms that abound in modern etiquette manuals are the graphic descriptions and detailed exhortations concerning bodily functions, dress, social relations, table manners, etc., found, for example, in Erasmus' influential essay *De civilitate morum puerilium libellus* (On civility in children), first published in 1526. As this unique treatise vividly demonstrates, when the decorous sensibilities of a class or society are in the process of being awakened or changed, nothing can be taken for granted or left to chance.[31]

This extended digression reiterates, among other things, the salience of the spoken word in the process of apology. The offender must not only *be* sorry but also has to *say* so. In this area of human conduct, speech is the difference that makes all the difference in the world and that is most effective because of its revelatory character. Once we recognize that an apology is essentially a speech act, a number of apparent perplexities are resolved.[32]

For example, an apology cannot and does not attempt to accomplish anything outside of speech. But what this speech ultimately entreats from the other is exceptional and urgent: nothing less than forgiveness, redemption, and acceptance that serve to restore one's sense of reality and place in a moral order. As a particular form of revelatory discourse, an apology is emblematic of the offender's socially liminal, ambiguous status that places him precariously midway between exclusion (actual or threatened) and rehabilitation. The use of the term "rehabilitation" is deliberate and stresses the difference between an apology and a *rite of passage*, although the two are similar in some respects.[33] The crucial concern of an apology is not with new rights and obligations associated with a change in social status but rather with the reclamation and revalidation of those enjoyed prior to the discreditable transgression.[34] In this context, there is perhaps no clearer depiction of apology as a propitiatory overture to a poignant homecoming and reconciliation than the parable of the prodigal son in Luke 15: 11–32:

Jesus went on to say, "There once was a man who had two sons. The younger one said to him, 'Father, give me now my share of the property.' So the man divided the property between his two sons. After a few days the younger son sold his part of the property and left home with the money. He went to a country far away, where he wasted his money in reckless living. He spent everything he had. Then a severe famine spread over that country, and he was left without a thing. So he went to work for one of the citizens of that country, who sent him out to his farm to take care of the pigs. He wished he could fill himself with the bean pods the pigs ate, but no one gave him anything to eat. At last he came to his senses and said, 'All my father's hired workers have more than they can eat, and here I am, about to starve! I will get up and go to my father and say, "Father, I have sinned against God and against you. I am no longer fit to be called your son; treat me as one of your hired workers."'

So he got up and started back to his father.

"He was still a long way from home when his father saw him; his heart was filled with pity and he ran, threw his arms around his son, and kissed him. 'Father,' the son said, 'I have sinned against God and against you. I am no longer fit to be called your son.' But the father called his servants: 'Hurry!' he said. 'Bring the best robe and put it on him. Put a ring on his finger and shoes on his feet. Then get the prize calf and kill it, and let us celebrate with a feast! Because this son of mine was dead, but now he is alive; he was lost, but now he has been found.' And so the feasting began.

"The older son, in the meantime, was out in the field. On his way back, when he came close to the house, he heard the music and dancing. He called one of the servants and asked him, 'What's going on?' 'Your brother came back home,' the servant answered, 'and your father killed the prize calf, because he got back safe and sound.' The older brother was so angry that he would not go into the house; so his father came out and begged him to come in. 'Look,' he answered back to his father, 'all these years I have worked like a slave for you, and I never disobeyed your orders. What have you given me? Not even a goat for me to have a feast with my friends! But this son of yours wasted all your property on prostitutes, and when he comes back home you kill the prize calf for him!' 'My son,' the father answered, 'you are always here with me and everything I have is yours. But we had to have a feast and be happy, because your brother was dead, but now he is alive; he was lost, but now he has been found.'"

The definitive, yet aleatory, nature of such a redemptive project helps to explain why other forms of communication serve, at best, as auxiliaries. Their participatory potency simply cannot match that of the unmediated presence of the spoken word demanded by the purgative ordeal of apology. So, too, acts of penance and restitution, tears, downcast looks, promises, and other emotive expressions, though often accompaniments of apology and useful as symbolic seals of the renewed covenant, are but accoutrements once we come to see that its central idea and purpose is to convey sorrow through speech. That we, as active participants in this mysterious undertaking, manage to recognize and recollect something crucial accomplished by that speech is a remarkable human achievement.

Apology as Social Exchange

Further enhancing the thaumaturgical aura of apology are the para-doxical ways in which it is circumscribed, but not ultimately ruled, by the language of commercial exchange and conventional notions of rational self-interest. In English, at least, we commonly say that one "owes," "gives," "offers," "receives," "accepts," etc., an apology, implying thereby that something almost tangible is being bartered. Furthermore, norm violations usually activate the strongest possible self-interest in the sense that most people are strongly motivated to conceal, deny, or rationalize their violations. In the case of apology, however, the meanings of "consideration" and "self-interest" are radically transformed. For example, in the model letters cited earlier, the offenders voluntarily come forward to seek forgiveness after having violated what they and their interlocutors took for granted as a morally binding condition of friendship. But what, we may ask, is offered in exchange? Curiously, *nothing*, except a self-abnegating speech expressing regret. So contrary to the logic of the economic marketplace or conceptions of social exchange based upon exclusively rational calculation, the apology itself—without any other objective consideration—constitutes both the medium of exchange and the symbolic quid pro quo for, as it were, "compensation."[35]

In this respect, although excuses, defenses, disclaimers, and justifi-cations are also speech acts whose very utterances seek to effect, they differ structurally from apologies taken as social exchanges in two major ways. First, as stated earlier, they offer the harmed party *some-thing*, for example, an external contingency or impaired capacity, in return not for remission but rather for understanding and exonera-tion. Second, the question of membership status may, but does not necessarily, arise in situations where accounts are pivotal. By contrast, and as indicated etymologically, to apologize is to bear free witness to the fact that one had no excuse, defense, or justification and that something more than credibility or understanding is at stake.

These differences also suggest that one who gives an account asks the other to be reasonable by virtue of a reason that either partially or totally denies authorship of an act. But the one who apologizes

asks forgiveness and, by extension, absolution from that which is unreasonable, unwarranted, and for which one is patently undeserving.
Consequently, when we apologize, we are in the morally unsettling
position of seeking unconditional pardon precisely in the context of
our being categorically unworthy. Aside from this poignant dilemma,
the offender's speech must also guard against the ever-present and
inviting tendency of an apology to degenerate into a perverse form of
exhibitionism, self-pity, or, as previously noted in passing, egocentric
indulgence.[36]

In these terms, the heart of an apology consists of a speech act
that responds to a compelling call about something that can neither
be forgotten nor forsaken. And although commercial metaphors are
preeminent (and heuristically useful) in the discursive domain of
apology, they can only approximate the intricacies of this form of
social interaction. Specifically, the morally asymmetrical positions
of the protagonists, the essentially symbolic character of the transaction, and the unpredictability of the outcome are among the crucial
elements of the process that are not easily explicated by elementary
conceptions of reciprocity. Furthermore, as already noted, although
pledges to honor previously unstated grounds of our agreements
with others, promises not to repeat the offense, etc., may be proffered or even demanded as tokens of good faith, they are, at best,
superfluous and, at worst, harmful to the overall project of apology.
Superfluous because the violation is irreversible (though *not* irre-
parable), and potentially damaging, since they invite close scrutiny
of commitments whose intrinsic force resides in their unstipulated,
axiomatic, and self-evident status.

We are faced, then, with an apparently enigmatic situation in
which the offender asks forgiveness as the necessary and symbolic
corrective for a harmful action on the flimsiest of grounds: a speech
act that is predicated upon the impossibility of restitution. Needless
to argue, a culturally nurtured sensibility that countenances apology
must also subscribe to the concept of forgiveness while suppressing
the impulse to retaliate in kind or, as is more likely given the emotional potential inherent in grave transgressions, to give back more
than was received in the absence of juridical redress.

Carried to its moral conclusion, an apology may be taken to represent the institutionalization of symbolic exchange as one means of precluding or containing socially disruptive conflicts. The latter would settle matters at one level, but at the cost of charging social relations with enormous tensions that could lead to their permanent severance or a permanent state of enmity. This state of affairs is most clearly revealed in societies that stress personal, familial, and institutional honor, although it is by no means limited to such societies. According to one anthropological account, for example, among the contentious and proud Greek-speaking Sarakatsani shepherds apologies are recognized but rare for settling disputes, dealing with insults, and remedying other conflicts:

Self-regard is a subjective and personal sentiment. At the same time the situations which provoke it are socially defined. All those elements of prestige, whether of the individual or the family, affect it and are sanctioned by it. A man's self-regard leads him to conserve his honour, to act honourably, to strive after wealth, to act proudly and arrogantly and so on. Self-regard inhibits any conduct on which an interpretation of weakness may be placed. For instance, the Sarakatsani seldom accept or give apologies. "A pardon is not acceptable" (*den pianetai to parnton*), it is said.[37]

There is a further important implication in the high paradox of receiving (or seeking) unmerited forgiveness of indefensible actions. Namely, that apology stands in relation to what is considered just and equitable by reminding us that if we had resort only to accounts or legal sanctions in our dealings with others, civilized life would be greatly diminished or rendered impossible.[38]

The cost of the uniquely human achievement of moving from material, behavioral, or legal to symbolic exchanges in the realm of personal transgressions is not inconsiderable for either party. Responding to the call for an apology and the process this sets in motion can be as painful and devastating as, if not worse than, any form of physical retribution. Once the symbolic overture has been made, the victim alone holds the keys of redemption and reconciliation. But this power also entails a profound moral obligation since the helpless offender, *in consideration for nothing more than a speech*, asks for nothing less than the conversion of righteous indignation and betrayal into unconditional forgiveness and reunion.

Finally, forgiveness itself involves a radical affective alternation, which, as Simmel suggests in his discussion of conciliation, may occur independently of an appeal or as an expression of volition:

Its [conciliability] psychological and sociological character seems most closely akin to that of forgiving (*Verzeihen*). After all, forgiving, too, does not presuppose any laxity of reaction or lacking strength of antagonism. It too is lit up in all its purity after the most deeply felt wrong and the most passionate struggle. Hence in both conciliation and forgiving lies something irrational, something like a denial of what one still was a moment before. This mysterious rhythm of the soul which makes processes of this type depend precisely and exclusively on the processes which contradict them is perhaps most clearly revealed in forgiving. For forgiving is probably the only affective process which we assume without any question to be subordinate to the will—otherwise, the *begging* of forgiveness would be meaningless. A request can only move us to something over which the will has power. That I spare the vanquished enemy or renounce all revenge on the individual who has offended me, can understandably be achieved on the basis of a request: it depends on my will. But that I *forgive* them, that is, that the feeling of antagonism, hatred, separateness yield to another *feeling*—in this respect, a mere resolution seems to be as powerless as it is in respect to feelings generally. Actually, however, the situation is different, and cases where we *cannot* forgive even with our best will are very rare.[39]

Our linguistic point of departure has led us along some familiar but anfractuous paths in quest of understanding the nature of apology. What conclusions, however tentative, may be drawn at this stage of the journey? If I am at all correct in what I have been saying, apology has two fundamental requirements: the offender has to be sorry and has to say so. These are the essential elements of an authentic apology.[40] Other features, for example, offers of reparation, self-castigation, shame, embarrassment, or promises to reform, may accompany an apology, but they are inessential because, I submit, they are implicit in the state of "being sorry." Moreover, unless carefully tendered, such professions can easily drown out the voice of sorrow and compromise the unconditionality required of forgiveness. Whatever else is said or conveyed, an apology must express sorrow. If the injured party believes that the offender is genuinely sorry, additional reassurances are superfluous. In some arcane way, then, one's future actions come to be seen as immanent in the evanescent speech that expresses one's present sorrow and regret.[41]

Apology in Japan and the West

The miraculous properties of apology and exquisite nuances of the offender-offended nexus are perhaps nowhere more clearly delineated than in Japan, the apologetic society par excellence. The regulative and symbolic functions of apology here clearly merit a study of their own as well as an acute ethnolinguistic sensitivity. To my knowledge, there is no monograph on this topic available in English, although various sources contain useful references and commentaries on apology. Consequently, I shall do little more than touch upon this powerful theme as a means of elaborating our analysis of apology and, to a lesser extent, contrasting Japanese and Western patterns. For these purposes, the work of the psychiatrist Takeo Doi guides the discussion.[42]

In the course of questioning Ruth Benedict's characterization of Japan as a shame culture rather than a guilt culture, Doi asserts, "The Japanese sense of guilt . . . shows a very clearcut structure, commencing as it does with betrayal [of the members of one's group] and ending in apology; it represents, in fact, the very prototype of the sense of guilt, and Benedict's failure to see this can only be attributed to her cultural prejudice."[43] He goes on to give the following anecdotal accounts of the potency and efficacy of an apology in Japan, even when it is expressed unintentionally:

It is very interesting in this connection that Father Heuvers, who has been in Japan ever since the Great Kanto Earthquake of 1923, should have written of his realization of the magical power of apology in Japan. It is particularly noteworthy that a Christian missionary, who came to Japan to preach forgiveness of sin, should have been so impressed by the realization that among Japanese a heartfelt apology leads easily to reconciliation. I am sure that other foreigners in Japan beside Fr. Heuvers have noticed the same thing, and it may well be this that has given rise to the popular theory that the Japanese have a poor sense of guilt.

An episode that I heard from an American psychiatrist will also serve to back up the observations of Fr. Heuvers just described. Through some oversight in carrying out immigration formalities, he found himself being hauled over the coals by an official of the Immigration Bureau. However often he explained that it was not really his fault, the official would not be appeased until, at the end of his tether, he said "I'm sorry . . ." as a prelude to a further argument, whereupon the official's expression suddenly changed and he dismissed the matter without further ado. The "I'm sorry" that he had used was far from being the same as the Japanese apologetic use of *sumanai* [a term that expresses both gratitude and apology] but the official had obviously taken it as this apologetic *sumanai*. The psychiatrist in question told me this story as an instance of the oddity of the Japanese people, but one might, of course, equally see it as an example of the peculiarity of the Western psychology, since people in the West, despite Benedict's description of them as inhabitants of a culture of guilt—or, one may say a little cynically, precisely because of that—are generally speaking reluctant to apologize. This is something that has gradually come to be recognized as the number of Japanese with experience of travel abroad has increased.[44]

I shall return to Doi's contention about the reluctance of Westerners to apologize later, but his general point is neatly reiterated by another, more notorious, encounter between a foreigner and Japanese authorities:

Ex-Beatle Paul McCartney headed for Britain yesterday apparently none the worse for his 10 days in a Japanese jail cell for a marijuana investigation. The 37-year-old rock superstar boarded a jetliner after Japanese prosecutors decided to deport him instead of charging him with marijuana possession— a charge that could have led to a seven-year prison sentence. . . . Japanese authorities said they decided to release him because he had "been punished enough." He had "shown signs of repentance and apologized," they said, and had told them the marijuana was for his "private use." The prosecutors took into consideration another factor, Kyodo said—"cancellation of his scheduled 11-concert performance." The cancellation cost millions of dollars in ticket sales.[45]

Doi argues that the call for apology in Japan emanates from two sources: fear and guilt. While fear-apology provides us with insights into a mentality quite alien to our own and contributes to the impression that Japanese apologize more often than Westerners, guilt-apology is more germane to our inquiry because the former is routinely employed in situations where no questionable action has occurred. To the contrary, in the case of fear-apology the person who "apologizes" has benefited from the action of another and uses the word *sumanai*, which, according to Doi, expresses *both* gratitude and apology. Whereas a Westerner would respond with an expression of gratitude, such as "thank you very much" or some variant depending on the circumstances, the social-psychological implications for the Japanese are apparently more complicated:

The question here, however, is why the Japanese are not content simply to show gratitude for a kind action but must apologize for the trouble which they imagine it has caused the other person. The reason is that they fear that unless they apologize the other man will think them impolite with the result that they may lose his good will. And this, it seems, accounts for the frequency of the word *sumanai*—the desire not to lose the other's good will, to be permitted the same degree of self-indulgence [*amae*] indefinitely.[46]

By contrast, a guilt-apology follows the sequence consistent with the "Western" pattern we have identified as event, call, apology, forgiveness, reconciliation. The Japanese version of this paradigm also involves conduct that potentially signifies betrayal, jeopardizes a valued relationship, and evokes guilt as well as fear. Nevertheless, the event in question is socially certified as betrayal, that is, "apologizable," only when the offender admits guilt by using the word *sumanai*:

The word *sumanai* . . . serves as the most appropriate confession of the sense of guilt in such a case. Moreover, although the sense of guilt as such begins, one might say, when one has done something that one should not, the general view is that there is no admission of one's guilt unless the misdeed is accompanied by a feeling of *sumanai*. The sense of guilt summed up in the word *sumanai* naturally connects up with the actual act of apology.[47]

These comments and observations serve, once more, to remind us of the immense power of the spoken word and that an apology is essentially a speech act with profound effects, when the words do indeed affect.

There are two other threads of Doi's discussion that correspond to apology in the West and thus merit our attention. The first has to do with the link between taking responsibility for one's actions and a sense of control over one's life, destiny, or social environment. In this moral context, an offender who apologizes too often or easily may subvert the project and raise doubts about his or her motives by crossing the fine line that separates apologies from excuses. The pattern not only fails to bring matters to a satisfactory conclusion but also places the offender in the position of seeming to ask carte blanche. As Doi points out:

It is interesting that people should be far keener on apologizing in Japan, where the sense of shame is highly developed, than in the West, which is supposed to be a culture of guilt. It is not merely that in Japan the individual says *sumanai* of something that is already done and finished. The Japanese also tend to stress their own lack of power to control what they will do from now on—which is tantamount to an apology, in advance, i.e., an excuse. Indeed, the Japanese apology very frequently has, in itself, a ring of self-excuse, a result of the fact that the Japanese sense of guilt includes a considerable admixture of the sense of shame from the very beginning. Generally speaking, the apology *sumanai* is aimed at not losing the other's good will. There is no problem when the feeling of being in the wrong is obviously genuine, but it sometimes happens that the person who repeats *sumanai* with too much facility is rebuffed with the reply *sumanai de sumu to omou ka* (literally, "do you think that to say 'it is not finished' will finish it?" i.e., facile apology is not enough).[48]

I do not know of any inquiries that have sought to explore the connections between control (actual or perceived) over one's social circumstances and the propensity to apologize. Nevertheless, I suspect that Doi's observations (including those concerning guilt and shame) can be generalized. Specifically, they suggest that individuals and collectivities lacking a sense of autonomy and, by extension, a firm social identity are likely to apologize promiscuously and excessively. For example, in North American culture we would expect this kind of defensive and propitiatory reaction among those who habitually experience extended social blackouts such as alcohol and drug abusers, as well as oppressed, stigmatized, or marginal groups and categories such as (where applicable) racial, ethnic, and religious minorities, colonized peoples, homosexuals, and other social subordinates. In all of these cases, assuming the putative relationship holds, apologies are intimately related to the problematics of membership status of one kind or another, whatever else is at stake.[49]

Second, Doi emphasizes the importance of the offender's dependent stance and its effect on the injured party's response:

The word *sumanai* usually includes a plea for the good will of the other party, and the same is true of *moshiwake nai* (literally, I have no excuse). In other words, it is an expression of a desire to be forgiven even though the relationship as such is not one where *amae* [self-indulgence] would normally apply. It is this, probably—the way in which, in Japan an apology comprises what is essentially a child-like plea to the other party, and the fact that this attitude is always received sympathetically—that gives the apology its magical efficacy in foreign eyes.[50]

What is of particular interest to us here is not so much the expression of helplessness without a legitimate claim to an *amae* relationship, that is, one that fulfills the need or desire for self-indulgence, but the reference to childhood. If the usage "child-like" is interpreted in the metaphoric context of vulnerability as well as dependency (although the two may overlap), then it highlights a generic and paradoxical aspect of apology in its Western version. As emphasized throughout, when we, as adult members, respond to a call and apologize, we proclaim our defenselessness and thus are literally at the mercy of the other. But for an apology to touch and quicken the compassionate sensibilities of the injured party—to work its magic, in Doi's terms—we must renounce all defenses, including that of puerility.

Now this can be an extremely delicate proposition because to claim (or even intimate) this exemption—often a tempting strategy—would effectively invalidate the criterion of unqualified responsibility that is essential to apologetic speech, cast doubt upon the offender's understanding of and, derivatively, moral commitment to the rule, and thus allow for the conversion of the apology into an account.[51] The point is that for an apology to be taken (and given) seriously in North American society, at least, a "child-like" plea, in and by itself, cannot adequately discharge the conjoint obligations of an informed response *to* the call and assuming responsibility *for* one's conduct. As a consequence, the offender has, among other things, to assume such a stance but without the corresponding unaccountability typically ascribed to a social and moral fledgling. "Child-like," in other words, must be a metaphor for self-imposed exposure and not for innocence.[52]

We come, finally, to the interrelated questions of the relative frequency and forms of apology in the Occident and Japan. Needless to say, one cannot ignore the larger setting in which the meaning and discursive expression of apology are given coherence without risking a grossly distorted view of things. Obviously, the social-psychological import of this speech act will differ in a culture where it is habitually expected and tendered in contrast to one in which apologies appear to be less salient in everyday affairs. Precisely how is still not clear to me, although I suspect that the institutionalization of apologetic discourse has a tempering effect with respect to interpersonal and formal social controls. For example, in Japan, and this is undoubtedly an oversimplification, the primacy of the group and a strong sense of individual responsibility to significant and nurturant others can be oppressive as well as comforting. Apologies do not necessarily resolve these tensions, but they do mitigate them to the extent that they soften and humanize a demanding, hierarchical social system.

At the same time, I would take issue with Doi (and others) as to the purportedly greater penchant of the Japanese for apology in comparison with Westerners. This is a statement that is commonly asserted as fact rather than adduced and that requires qualification. My reservations are on the following grounds. First, if it were somehow possible to ascertain the proportion of "guilt" to "fear" apologies between individuals, Japanese probably would not show a significantly greater propensity to apologize in Occidental terms. Second, apart from the custom of apologizing (or, more accurately, using apologetic speech) when receiving a favor or good will—which does not qualify as an apology in North America—the lavish use of honorifics and attention to etiquette are likely to lend credence to the notion that apology is more common in Japan than elsewhere. Finally, and this takes us beyond the issue of frequency, the argument is supported by virtue of a category of apology that (until quite recently) has been uncommon in the West. This consists of the widespread practice of apologies by private and public corporate entities to individuals whom they have harmed or wronged. Although we shall consider this form in greater detail in the following chapter, some brief comments are now in order to conclude our discussion of Japanese-Occidental similarities and differences.

In Western societies, individuals who are unable or unwilling to express sorrow and regret after knowingly harming someone are ordinarily viewed as doubly deviant and subject to sanctions according to the dominant form of discourse and social control, for example, custom, codified law, religion, medicine, or politics.[53] By contrast, corporations, formal organizations, institutions, and other synthetic social creatures are generally not bound by this moral imperative. Were an officer, corporation, or public agency charged with questionable, illegal, or harmful activities to call a press conference and announce, "We are sorry this happened and wish to apologize for our role in . . . ," they would certainly be subject to subsequent legal liabilities and penalties. In this respect, corporations and similarly constituted collectivities are sociopathic: they are incapable, on the whole, of acknowledging regret and expressing remorse.[54]

Japanese corporations and bureaucracies are certainly not immune to corruption, scandal, or wrongdoing, whether the latter be intentional or accidental. Nevertheless, unlike their Western counterparts, and this is a crucial difference, they are much more likely to be active participants in the moral economy of apology. Consider, for example, the following account of what is not an unusual occurrence:

The president of the Japan Nuclear Power Company apologized for accidents, saying his company had undermined the Government's policy of replacing oil with "clean nuclear energy."[55]

Or, more dramatically, after the bloody massacre at Israel's Lod Airport in 1972 by three young Japanese radicals, it was reported:

A stream of delegations, mostly of young people, called at the Israeli embassy in Tokyo to apologize. Kyoto University President Toshio Maeda, summoned to the Ministry of Education, bowed low to express regret and admit that he was "at a loss how to apologize to the nation for the fact that two of the three culprits had been students at our university." Education Minister Saburo Takami, in turn, apologized for the shortcomings of the educational system, while Foreign Minister Takeo Fukuda spoke of the dishonor to the nation. In each case, the appropriate official was following an ages-old tradition of "taking responsibility" that has evolved from the Japanese family system. Even the nation is considered a family, headed by the Tenno or Emperor. If one member stains the family reputation, his relatives are expected to make a show of remorse and expiation. In Jerusalem, Japanese Ambassador Eiji Tokura appeared on television. "Dear citizens of Israel," he said in halting Hebrew, "it is my wish to express my sorrow and apologize for this terrible crime perpetrated by Japanese nationals." Then he burst into tears.[56]

The humanizing and civilizing potential of apology, for individuals and institutions, is a theme that we shall encounter at many points of our inquiry. This chapter has raised more questions than it has answered, or come close to illuminating, and it is now time to examine our speculations more systematically and empirically. As a first step in this direction, let us consider various forms of apology, focusing upon the social units involved in this deceptively simple but significant moral enterprise.

3. *Modes of Apology (1)*

B*y now we have seen* that apology, or, more aptly, apologetic speech, is a decisive moment in a complex restorative project arising from an unaccountable infraction and culminating in remorse and reconciliation. Each stage of the process (which may take a minute or a lifetime) confronts the co-participants with moral choices that cumulatively serve to move them toward amity and reunion or hostility and estrangement. As with any human endeavor whose realization is constrained by dialectical reciprocity—the temporary unity of an intricate pas de deux comes immediately to mind—each phase is acutely susceptible to miscalculation, impasse, uncertainty, and failure to achieve desired ends. Hence, the process may be stillborn if the original transgression is considered to be beyond redemption; the speech act itself may be defective, ill-timed, or disqualified on other grounds; sorrow may give way to pride, or guilt to anger; forgiveness may be withheld, conditional, or granted without subsequent reconciliation, thus marking the end of the relationship; some kind of rapprochement may be established but without forgiveness, and so on. Given such disabling contingencies, the uselessness of accounts as defenses, the potential pain and torment of moral vulnerability, the possibility of social ostracism, the attraction of retaliation and revenge, and the unpredictability and particularity of forgiveness—in short, the apparently overwhelming odds against success—the resort to apology emerges as a remarkable response to the obstinate facts of moral trespass and malice in human affairs.[1]

Earlier, we touched upon some of the distinctive characteristics of the apologetic mode, for example, how its speech differs from that of accounts, the theoretical status of the offender, the problematics of membership in the face of moral transgression, and the severity of the offense. In the next chapter, we shall look more closely at various forms of apology in which collectivities are implicated. But before considering these, some extended prefatory remarks are in order regarding a number of related but distinguishable questions that, until now, have been dealt with in passing. Specifically, these are the essential interactional principle of apology, the role of third parties, and the pedagogy of apology. This approach will provide us with occasions for clarifying and qualifying our theoretical assertions and generalizations. My sources in what follows, as throughout this inquiry, are necessarily eclectic and often fugitive, including a mélange of journalistic, literary, and other available materials that, in some way or another, illuminate the social significance of apology.

The Essential Interactional Principle of Apology

At the outset, it should be noted that whatever the actual or conceptual status of the relevant units (individuals, corporate entities, or collectivities), *the fundamental pattern of sociation in apologetic discourse is dyadic.* That is to say, its exclusive, ultimate, and ineluctable focus is upon interaction between the primordial social categories of Offender and Offended. This means that it cannot be understood in terms of one party to the exclusion of the other. By the same token, while third parties may enter into the proceedings at one point or another, have a stake in the outcome, and so on, they remain, even in their most influential capacities, peripheral to the critical field of interaction. To put it yet another way, the bedrock structure of apology is binary, a product of a relationship between the Offender and the Offended that can neither be reduced nor augmented without undergoing a radical metamorphosis.

Hannah Arendt's remarks on what she calls the condition of plurality and the faculties of forgiving and promising cogently speak to the issue of reduction and apply with equal force to apology:

> Both faculties . . . depend on plurality, on the presence and acting of others, for no one can forgive himself and no one can feel bound by a promise made only to himself; forgiving and promising enacted in solitude and isolation remain without reality and can signify no more than a role played before one's self.[2]

So, too, apology is a relational concept and practice that necessarily requires an individual or collective Other to realize itself. It is an externalized speech act whose meaning resides not within the individual (although its effects may), but in a social bond between the Offender and Offended, no matter who else knows of the wrong that created it. And it is a relationship that, paradoxically, must be abrogated in order to secure itself.[3]

Following Arendt's lead, we may ask if it makes any sense to speak of apology in the context of auto-infidelities or violations of one's own ideals, beliefs, or principles? I think not. Examples of self-apology (as opposed to self-pity), a situation that would entail the merging of the Offender-Offended statuses, are hard to come by except, perhaps, in poesy and psychopathology. On a more mundane level, in our everyday affairs, it seems that self-apology involves an intractable contradiction: an almost unbearable tension that calls for a sharp separation of self and experience (or reality) that is difficult to sustain, no less resolve. Thus apology is ruled out, has no place in the absence of an offended other, and can appear only as a chimerical caricature of the original in one's solipsistic reveries. We are left, finally, with a sense of guilt, shame, cynicism, or despair to assuage our self-inflicted disquiet and pain.

Forgiveness, as Arendt reminds us, also is deprived of its vital spirit and grounds in the absence of others, but somewhat differently than apology. Conventional, unreflective speech furnishes some insights into these matters. Consider, for example, the idiomatic usage, "I cannot (will, never, etc.) forgive myself for . . . ," when someone is referring to a self-violation. By contrast, the affirmative version, "I can (do, will, etc.) forgive myself for . . . ," the formulation Arendt's argument addresses, is comparatively uncommon. Moreover, to my knowledge, there is no linguistic/semantic equivalent in English, at least, for expressing reflexive apology, either positively or negatively. In other words, unless apology is directed outward, it becomes incomprehensible. What I am suggesting here is that apology presents us with a distinct form of discourse, social par excellence, with unremitting demands that cannot be satisfied by internal monologue. Self-apology and self-forgiveness (with the exceptions noted) remain, at best, spurious achievements in hermetic worlds.

From a purely formal or taxonomic perspective, then, the dualistic axiom generates four structural configurations of apology (and forgiveness) with respect to the units of interaction:

1. Interpersonal apology from one individual to another, or *One to One*.
2. Apology from an individual to a collectivity, or *One to Many*.
3. Apology from a collectivity to an individual, or *Many to One*.
4. Apology from one collectivity to another, or *Many to Many*.

Because we have already dealt at length with interpersonal apology, our primary concern in what follows shall be with the other three forms. Although these are less frequently encountered in Western culture as opposed to interpersonal apology, they—and especially the One to Many and Many to One patterns—are important for deepening our understanding of this discourse for two reasons. First, they highlight and underscore potential tensions between individual integrity and group solidarity. Second, and I shall have much more to say about this in the following chapter, these types not only recapitulate the basic elements of interpersonal apology but also elaborate them by accentuating and extending the essentially *public* character of apologetic discourse. (The situation of Many to Many apology raises another set of questions that will be addressed later.) In these interactional contexts, the presence of a collective Offender or Offended introduces new elements into the dialogue without thereby altering the dyadic equation. As a consequence, shame, guilt, anger, humiliation, exposure, and membership, all of which enter into One to One apology, take on added significance.

The typology proposed is not merely a matter of definitional fiat but follows directly from the discursive properties of the apologetic mode. As I have tried to show, an authentic apology cannot be delegated, consigned, exacted, or assumed by the principals, no less outsiders, without totally altering its meaning and vitiating its moral force. This observation seems clear enough when we are dealing with transgressions in the One to One category. As the offender, for example, I cannot have someone apologize on my behalf any more than I, as the offended, can forgive by proxy or have another bestow this gift without my knowledge or consent.[4] At the interpersonal level, therefore, others are not usually empowered to discharge our moral obligations, although they may not be deterred from trying to do so when what we have done or suffered rebounds to their benefit or detriment.[5] To request, encourage, allow, or be subjected to such mediatory actions violates both the logic and spirit of apology, shifts its moral trajectory, raises questions about competence and responsibility, and tends to move all concerned into the realm of accounts. Such interventions are, in short, self-defeating and antithetical to the apologetic agenda, which calls for direct exchanges between particular wrongdoers and their victims.

Or so it would seem.

But when individuals are members of highly solidary groups and collectivities, things can become much more complicated.[6] At first glance, our earlier example of the Lod Airport massacre apparently refutes (or strongly qualifies) the dyadic principle insofar as parties other than the actual perpetrators assumed the obligation to apologize. To the contrary, a closer inspection of this and similar incidents adds further confirmation to the validity of the dualistic structure of apology. The Japanese authorities, far from accepting the ontological status of third parties, defined themselves as symbolic co-offenders.[7] As such, and as custodians of national honor, they were able to transform the individual responsibility of the terrorists into a collective one. Difficult as it may be for the Western mentality to comprehend, the whole culture (in a manner of speaking) accepted blame for what three of its members had done and thus nullified the concept of third parties.

Needless to say, this practice is neither universal nor widespread, does not require the concurrence or even presence of the wrong-doers, and where present supplements rather than replaces One to One apology. It is most commonly found in what has been termed "honor-sensitive" societies and in cultures where group or collective membership, interests, and claims, as well as institutionalized hierarchical arrangements, take precedence over individuality and egalitarianism, as they clearly do in Japan and other settings. Finally, this pattern is likely to be found in situations where concerned individuals or groups seek through some kind of symbolic reparation to redress past wrongs or injuries committed by other members. But in the absence of these conditions, I would argue, the ability of those not directly involved to enforce judgments, impose sanctions, command contrition, or proffer forgiveness is sharply delimited, if non-existent.

Apology and Third Parties

At the same time, to stress the dyadic and unmediated character of apology is not to discount the potential moral and coercive influence of third parties. This is so because normative violations only rarely remain private or without wider social resonance. Assuming some knowledge of the transgressive circumstances, third parties may position themselves in a number of ways vis-à-vis the offender, offended, and offense. First, and perhaps most obviously, they may move closer to the field of action or away from it. Some of the more common and potentially significant roles of the third party, so to speak, include Casual Bystander, Impartial Observer, Eyewitness, Commentator, Critic, Conciliator, Mediator, Advocate, Adjudicator, and Judge. These categories (and their associated activities), it should be noted, are not necessarily mutually exclusive, fixed, or universal but are more or less institutionalized in cultures that recognize and use apology as a means of resolving disagreements and conflicts. Second, depending upon their relations with the protagonists, their own interests and values, or broader moral questions arising from the infraction, such actors may serve to certify an offense as apologizable, add their voices in the call for apology, urge its acceptance or rejection, appraise matters of form and timing, and judge the sincerity of remorse and forgiveness.

What is less patent, but consequential, given the ultimate executive impotence of third parties, is how their participation in *any* capacity introduces new elements and dynamics into the offender-offended relationship. Such intervention, whether intentional, spontaneous, or accidental, typically militates against a mutually acceptable and morally satisfying resolution insofar as it interferes with the normal unfolding of the process or shifts the grounds of discourse so as to include other issues. But what is of crucial structural import here is the conversion of what was a relatively private, dyadic conflict between the two parties, sequestered from outsiders, into a public dispute involving specific others with interests and commitments of their own.[8]

But there is much more to it than this. This intervention of third parties (by invitation, imposition, accident, or choice), apart from expanding the universe of discourse and, hence, laying bare intimate details of wrongdoing and discord to the scrutiny of others, has additional implications and consequences. In the first place, whatever the initial stance of external moral invigilators, be it conciliatory or admonitory, their very mobilization signals impasse, intransigence, and antagonism on the part of one or both principals. Second, as Gulliver points out with regard to the status of the mediator:

He becomes a party in the negotiations. He becomes a negotiator and as such, he inevitably brings with him, deliberately or not, certain ideas, knowledge, and assumptions, as well as certain interests and concerns of his own and those of other people whom he represents. Therefore he is not, and cannot be, neutral and merely a catalyst. He not only affects the interaction but, at least in part, seeks and encourages an outcome that is tolerable to him in terms of his own ideas and interests. He may even come into conflict with one or both of the parties.[9]

Given the fact that third parties always introduce, represent, or develop a third set of interests once they enter into the proceedings, apologies in such circumstances, if forthcoming, are likely in one way or another to become subject to standards the disputants themselves might otherwise not have applied.

Third, and of central importance, the participation of others is conducive to eliciting and exacerbating latent anger, self-righteousness, moral indignation, and, most perniciously, the development of a punitive atmosphere. There is, as I shall attempt to show, a strong propensity for third parties, willy-nilly, to inject into the apologetic dialogue an element utterly contrary to its purpose, alien to its spirit, and subversive of its power that can be roughly described as punitive moralizing. This is not necessarily punishment in the conventional sense, though certain material and symbolic penalties may constitute part of the reparative agenda set by others. What I am referring to is the humiliation of being pressed to admit a moral failing and show remorse for something that should have been settled voluntarily and without public intervention in the first place. In this context, what passes for a call is typically no more than barely disguised anger and the desire to chastise. Although punishment is a constant, if dormat, alternative to the moral logic of forgiveness, demand for it, more often than not, comes to the fore once apology receives public notice.[10]

The preceding considerations lead us, finally, to a related set of patterns generated, in part, by triadic interaction.[11] As we have suggested, when the call for apology moves from the private into the public realm, issues of honor, shame, pride, and conditions of membership become salient or of paramount importance. This is not to say that these are absent or inconsequential when the dialogue is carried on *in camera*, but that certain aspects of them become highlighted and magnified by the glare of publicity. One's conduct, for example, tends to become emblematic of more enduring social definitions and identities. There is, moreover, a concomitant temporal quickening or compression, a sense of urgency and impatience, pressure to move things along and conclude matters according to schedules that others view as reasonable or desirable. Disputants often discover that they are no longer free to control the pace of action and reaction or to put their conflict aside temporarily and attend to less stressful or rewarding aspects of the relationship. In sum, once others take part, there is some loss of personal sovereignty and flexibility on the part of one or both contestants.[12]

So, too, are points of honor, pride, and common decency raised at least implicitly in the course of dyadic apologetic speech. But here, assuming the situation is not beyond repair and the parties are genuinely committed to reconciliation, such questions tend to remain muted or are assessed within the total context and history of the relationship. They become central and ominously explicit, however, to the extent that third-party intervention shifts attention from the original trespass to the moral integrity of the interlocutors, in most cases that of the offender. This displacement comes about, in part, from the social incarnation of previously abstract and impersonal moral standards and codes that were either taken for granted as binding or deemed irrelevant to those directly involved. In other words, what was previously a Generalized Other to the offender and offended appears now as an embodied Particular Other. And because metrics of honor, repute, and prestige ultimately derive from community judgments, once a dyadic conflict is transformed into a public event in which third parties are implicated, questions of essential character and moral qualities arise. As a consequence, one's whole being becomes problematic rather than some specific discreditable action which, now exposed to other members, takes on a symptomatic meaning.[13]

Whatever the nature of the social relationship between the two parties (individuals or collectivities) and the circumstances surrounding the transgression that elicited the call for an apology, going public provides fresh opportunities for displays of pride, especially on the part of an irresolute or unresponsive offender. And, it should be added, turns all parties into performers. In the attempt to counter imputations of generic immorality and stigmatized membership status, save face, and avoid self-incrimination, the accused, now subject to public censure and entreaties, may resort to a number of defensive rhetorical strategies. Some of these include remaining silent, denying the allegations, challenging the validity of facts or interpretations, impugning the motives or authority of third parties, attempting to withdraw the matter from public discussion, or defending the action in question as accountable. Whether such measures succeed or fail—judgments that are rarely unproblematic when personal or collective pride and public censure are involved—they effectively redeploy issues of substance, character, and relationship into wider discursive domains while evoking coercive and punitive speech that contravenes apologetic speech and reconciliation.

Such inescapable generalities will become clearer once particulars are provided. Examples of the patterns I have been discussing abound in everyday life but are most pellucidly demonstrated in the fields of politics and international diplomacy. Let us therefore examine three notorious instances in which apologies and third parties figure prominently. The first concerns the Watergate affair and subsequent resignation of Richard M. Nixon as President of the United States during the early 1970s.

The bare facts of the matter are as follows. On 17 June 1972, five men were apprehended by police after attempting to enter and wiretap Democratic party national headquarters in the Watergate apartment complex in Washington, D.C. It was later discovered that this operation was part of a larger conspiracy involving political corruption, illegal wiretaps, corporate contributions in exchange for political favors, and other infractions on the part of Nixon, his closest associates, and members of the committee for the President's reelection. After televised hearings, indictments, convictions, and the initiation of impeachment proceedings during the following two years, on 9 August 1974 Nixon became the first President to resign while in office. Although senior advisers and officials in his administration were convicted and imprisoned, including H. R. Haldeman, John D. Ehrlichman, and John N. Mitchell, on 8 September 1974 Nixon received a pardon from his successor, Gerald R. Ford, for any crimes he might have committed while President.[14]

Although volumes have been and, no doubt, will continue to be written on Watergate and other enormities during the Nixon years, my concern here is with a seemingly small but, for our purposes, significant fact. And that is that Nixon never formally apologized to those he had wronged or to the nation for his complicities and abuse of office. As evidence of his crimes and attempts to obstruct investigations mounted prior to his resignation and after Ford's pardon, there was spirited public debate and contention about the possibilities of criminal prosecution, impeachment, imprisonment, amnesty, and other courses of action. At the same time, numerous and often vociferous calls came from friends and foes alike—private citizens, public officials, the media—for *at least* an apology as a token of contrition, remorse, and honesty. Nixon remained silent.

The closest he ever came to an apology, *and it was never taken as such by Nixon or anyone else*, was a classic display of equivocation in his speech of resignation televised to the nation on the evening of 8 August 1974. In his address, Nixon did not use the word "apology" once or mention specific charges that had been made against him but rather sought to explain his momentous decision on the grounds of a loss of congressional support for his policies, poor judgment, and errors committed in trying to serve higher national interests:

I regret deeply any injuries that may have been done in the course of events that led to this decision. I would say only that if some of my judgments were wrong, and some were wrong, they were made in what I believed at the time to be in the best interest of the Nation.[15]

Reflecting the generally restrained and sympathetic public response of the media, an editorial in the *New York Times* of 10 August 1974 noted:

Mr. Nixon is no stranger to defeat or adversity as he has reminded those around him frequently in these last days. It is unfortunate, however, that nowhere in his final public statement did there appear any acknowledgement that something about his own deeds in office might have justified his downfall. He remarked with obvious accuracy that he no longer had a strong enough political base in Congress to complete his term of office. But why had he lost that base?

It would have been easier for the nation to stress his accomplishments if he himself had shown more candor about his shortcomings.[16]

The sentiments expressed in Nixon's resignation speech were repeated one month later in his acceptance of Ford's "full, free and absolute pardon . . . for all offenses against the United States which he had committed or may have committed or taken part in" when he was President. They also provide us with an important key for understanding why an apology was not forthcoming:

No words can describe the depths of my regret and pain at the anguish my mistakes over Watergate have caused the nation and the Presidency. . . . I know that many fair-minded people believe that my motivation and actions . . . were intentionally self-serving and illegal. I now understand how my own mistakes and misjudgments have contributed to that belief and seemed to support it. . . . That the way I tried to deal with Watergate was the wrong way is a burden I shall bear for every day of the life that is left to me.[17]

Although Nixon's admission of deep "regret" and "pain" may appear to satisfy the formal requirements of an apology—only the most uncharitable would deny that he had suffered—it missed the mark on at least two counts. First, he never acknowledged what it was that he was sorry about. Second, what Nixon said he regretted, that is, the anguish he had caused the nation and so forth, had nothing to do with what was troubling and angering people: a betrayal of trust and the arrogant abuse of power.

When it became apparent that an apology, as commonly understood, was not going to be offered, the calls, when raised at all, took on a punitive tone and became indistinguishable from retributive speech. As his words and deeds suggest, Nixon interpreted such entreaties, and correctly so I would argue, not as authentic calls for reconciliation but as sanctimonious demands for further punishment and public humiliation. This baneful wedding of public anger and personal pride effectively ruled out the possibility of a genuine apology and forgiveness and thus fueled the mutual bitterness and mistrust that had developed over time.

As later events showed, Nixon's understanding of what was being asked of him was deeper than his grasp of the expressive conditions of authentic apology in American culture. He believed that his act of resignation was the symbolic equivalent and sufficient evidence of remorse and thereby released him from the obligations of having to acknowledge his transgression, *say* he was sorry, and ask for forgiveness. This conviction was clearly set forth in Nixon's own words in recounting Watergate on national television in April 1984:

Washington (CP)—Reflecting on Watergate almost a decade after the scandal, Richard Nixon says the break-in was illegal and a "very, very stupid thing to do."

In a new, paid retelling of his memoirs ranging over a number of topics Nixon still refused to apologize for the Watergate scandal.

Asked why during the two-year ordeal he did not go on television and say he had made a mistake and was sorry, Nixon replied to interviewer Frank Gannon:

"There's no way you could apologize or to say that you are sorry which could exceed resigning the presidency of the United States. That said it all. And I don't intend to say any more."[18]

One could easily dismiss these matters as minor footnotes in American political history or, if so inclined, cite them as further corroborations of Nixonian paranoia and infamy. But if we probe more deeply than these alternatives allow, our example (which, like all "examples," does much more than exemplify) provides some valuable insights into our topic. Coupled with a meticulously detailed and epic chronicle of offenses, we are presented with lethal doses of anger, fear, subterfuge, blundering, and, above all, pride or stupefying *hubris* that combined to silence the voices of apology and forgiveness.[19] In these morally convoluted circumstances, the idea of an apology would have been as extraordinary as any effect it might presumably have had on "healing the nation"—a theme that appeared in Nixon's resignation speech, his acceptance of the pardon, and in the media.

There is something else that should be mentioned here. As we have seen, a call for an apology entails, among other things, a description or documentation of the material facts and attendant circumstances of the offense. In this recounting, moreover, the offender comments about what occurred. In these terms, an apology attests to, validates, confirms, records, and also objectifies—to the extent that what it refers to is "objective" for all concerned parties—truth or an accurate view of social reality. What this means practically is that the transgressor, in addition to pleading guilty as charged without a defense, expressing remorse, etc., says or affirms, "Yes, this is what happened. I agree with the wronged party (and others) as to the facts of the case and how they are being interpreted." In other words, apologetic discourse presupposes cognitive and evaluative congruence in the form of shared definitions of the violation, its severity, history, and implications. Now although Nixon did not dispute the "facts" of Watergate (after all, his own taped words confirmed them), he never regarded his own actions as anything more than mistakes and misjudgments. Similarly, his resignation, or rather the meaning he attached to it, was simply the price one paid for making an error but not for committing a crime. More to the point, neither Nixon nor Ford ever specified what was being forgiven or remitted by the pardon. This omission not only ended the whole affair on an Alice-in-Wonderland note but effectively precluded an apology by technically eliminating its raison d'être.

Once the particulars of Watergate and other irregularities became incontrovertible, Nixon's pride and pardon (for offenses unknown) rendered the notion of apology, especially at the behest of hostile and unsympathetic third parties, superfluous, if not spurious and punitive.[20] In a sense, his silence simultaneously formulated and answered a fundamental question that virtually everyone, critics and supporters, had overlooked: what would an apology mean in the light of these events? Nixon's response, what he did not say as much as what he did, indicated that it was certainly *not* an apology that was being sought. Rather, what was couched in the language of apology was little more than an angry demand for a symbolic surcharge in the form of a humbling confession on top of the ultimate payment he had already made, his resignation. Thus his view of the situation, based upon a clear reading and understanding of the evidence, produced a logic that was self-affirming and irrefutable but one that prevented him from wiping the slate clean, at least formally. In his own fashion, then, Nixon managed to penetrate and resolve some of the mysterious ambiguities and susceptibilities posed by apologetic discourse, authentic and spurious. By equating apology with payment and punition, and an alternative interpretation of his position would be difficult to defend, Nixon demonstrated a keen comprehension of how the call can be adulterated by anger and, at the same time, totally negated the concepts of apology and forgiveness.

The second example of unsuccessful third-party intervention involved a tragic incident that had international repercussions. On

1 September 1983, a South Korean commercial airliner with 269 persons aboard apparently strayed into strategically sensitive Soviet territory en route from New York to Seoul. After being tracked for over two hours, the plane was shot down by a Soviet fighter. There were no survivors.[21]

When the fate of the airliner became known, there was an eruption of charges, countercharges, and denunciations by the United States, the Soviet Union, South Korea, other nations, and various civil aviation organizations. Further complications ensued because of the lack of information about circumstances that precipitated the attack, the fact that South Korea and the Soviet Union did not have diplomatic relations, and the deaths of a conservative congressman and other American citizens who had been passengers. On 2 September, President Reagan set the bellicose tone that characterized the mutually accusatory discourse during the next few months, using such epithets as "uncivilized," "barbarous," "criminal," and "callous" to describe the Soviet action.

Calls for an apology from the Soviet Union and clarification of the facts soon followed. The President of South Korea (Chun Doo) accused the Soviets of having committed a "barbarous act" and demanded "the truth" and an apology. Korea's foreign minister also demanded a public apology, full compensation for the loss of lives and property, and a guarantee that such an act would not be repeated. At first, the Soviets neither acknowledged that they had shot down the plane nor accepted responsibility for what had occurred. When it became clear that they had indeed done so, they claimed that the airliner was on a spying mission, the intrusion was preplanned and a provocation, and their pilots had tried to warn the crew before attacking. Later they defended their action on the grounds of national defense and mistaken identification of the plane as an American military reconnaissance craft. There was only a passing expression of regret in the official statement issued by the official Soviet press agency, Tass.

These revelations soon became the center of escalating political tensions between the United States and the Soviet Union. The official

American position was summarized in a statement by Undersecretary of State Lawrence Eagleburger calling for a verification of facts, an apology, and restitution:

The Soviet Union "continues to lie to the world." He said that the admission that a Soviet fighter shot down the Korean Air Lines plane came "only after the truth was known everywhere that the U.S.S.R. without any justification shot down an unarmed civilian airliner with 269 people aboard." Soviet claims that its forces tried to warn the plane were "not borne out by the facts," he added.

"The world community still needs straight answers," Eagleburger declared. "Decent respect for the opinion of mankind requires that the Soviet Union must provide a full accounting for its actions. It must make restitution for the victims and families, and it must cooperate with international efforts to investigate the tragedy and to recover its victims."[22]

There were numerous other calls in the same vein, as well as resolutions of condemnation and proposed sanctions, such as trade embargoes, cancellation of cultural exchange programs, and the temporary suspension of air service to and from the Soviet Union. None of these moved Soviet leader Yuri V. Andropov or other senior officials to apologize or to acknowledge that they were at fault. Instead, the Soviets responded to mounting criticism by stressing the integrity of Russian air space and maintaining that the airliner had been engaged in espionage. On 7 September 1983, Foreign Minister Andrei Gromyko tersely set forth the Kremlin's position and warned that any future incursions would be dealt with summarily and in the same way as the Korean:

We state: Soviet territory, the borders of the Soviet Union are sacred. No matter who resorts to provocations of that kind, he should know that he will bear the full brunt of responsibility for it.[23]

During the two weeks following the event, the *New York Times* ran a daily section on developments in "The Air Liner Crisis," as it was called. There were also numerous commentaries and analyses in other publications and mass media concerning the incident and its aftermath. When it became evident that the Soviets had no intention of apologizing, this issue became less salient in public discussions, and attention shifted to establishing the facts and recovering the bodies and plane. But the question of apology was not totally eclipsed by these pressing matters. The frustration, perplexity, and anger in the face of what Western journalists, at least, took as egregious hubris on the part of the Soviets (corresponding, in many ways, to how the media reacted to Nixon and Watergate) was revealed on two occasions.

The first was a *New York Times* editorial (21 September 1983). After chiding the Reagan administration for "moving from dignified, justified anger toward political opportunism," it went on to say:

Yet angry Americans are, justifiably so. The Soviet Government's long hesitation before admitting the deed compounded its irresponsibility. The crude campaign to shift blame, as if any provocation could justify such murder, is more enraging still.

By what perverse values would even guiltless perpetrators shout defiance at the aggrieved? Even if the Soviet leaders thought they had a right to shoot, can't they bring themselves to say they're sorry?

There is no end of theories about how the paranoid Soviet psyche and bureaucracy habitually turn fear, shame and guilt into aggression. But it does not matter much, finally, whether such conduct is evil or sick or stupid. Our first, and mutual, problem in the nuclear age is survival.

Similar, but even more pointed, sentiments were expressed by another journalist, who interpreted the Soviet reaction as indicative of a fundamental moral impoverishment. In making his case, the writer touches upon several points that engaged us earlier:

There is a wisdom beyond sentimentality in the authentic apology. It has a purpose. Disraeli once said, "Apologies only account for that which they do not alter." That still accounts for much, and the accounting is indispensable. Perhaps not within a nation, where the law presumably does the accounting among individuals: the law pronounces judgment to mark an end to the cycle of vengeance that would otherwise follow a crime. But between nations there is no comparable agency to prevent historical wounds from festering endlessly. Nothing, except the apology. In an almost miraculous way, it seems capable of binding wounds. . . .

This is what makes the case of Korean Air Lines Flight 007 and the apology that never was so puzzling. The Soviets are not naive. They value public opinion and know how to manipulate it. After an initial stonewall, they . . . could not dispute the basic facts of the case. And they quickly became aware that they were suffering even more political damage from their lack of remorse than from shooting down the plane in the first place. As the cover of *The Economist* somewhat plaintively pointed out to Yuri Andropov, "You have nothing to lose by saying sorry." Yet he would not . . . .

For what was so stunning about the Soviet response was its *lack* of feeling. What sent a chill through the world . . . was the undertone of stony incomprehension in the Soviet response to pleas for some acknowledgement of responsibility. One sensed the absence of a certain faculty: a heart grown so cold that it had lost the capacity for remorse.

For an individual or a society, that capacity is a sign of life, of vitality, of a soul that can still be moved.[24]

To speak of a lack of feeling in this context may strike one as naive or mawkish given the atrocities routinely committed by various political regimes in this century. But for our purposes, the merit of Krauthammer's interpretation is not the issue. What seems more to the point, as with Nixon's reaction to Watergate, is the moral climate or sensibility required for authentic and effective apologetic discourse. Specifically, I am suggesting that apology cannot come about and do its work under conditions where the primary function of speech is defensive or purely instrumental and where legalities take precedence over moral imperatives. Once apology is defined as merely a pawn or gambit in a power game, it becomes part of another moral economy in which individuals or nations find little to be gained by apologizing for their transgressions as opposed to remaining silent, counterattacking, or trying to cut their losses to a minimum. To recognize this possibility is not necessarily to succumb to indifferent cynicism but to be reminded of the ancient precept *corruptio optimi pessima*—the corruption of the best is the worst.

Our final example concerns a covert Central Intelligence Agency operation in Canada during the late 1950s in which unsuspecting and unconsenting psychiatric patients were subjected to consciousness-altering drugs and experiments. A newspaper columnist succinctly described the situation as follows:

From 1957 to 1960, the CIA provided nearly $60,000 to Montreal psychiatrist, Ewen Cameron, for a series of mind-control experiments. These tests on nine Canadian victims, who are suing the CIA for $1-million each, were part of a post-Korean War investigation of brainwashing techniques. The victims suffered severe mental anguish from such psychiatric tricks as "psychic driving," electric shocks and experimental drugs. The CIA, according to documents secured by The Globe's Freedom of Information Act, tried hard to keep its involvement secret. The CIA was Dr. Cameron's only source of money from April, 1957, to June, 1960. The CIA then dropped out, leaving the U.S. Air Force to pick up part of the tab.

The courts can decide how Dr. Cameron's unfortunate patients should be recompensed, but no one can argue that they were not sorely done by. Leaving monetary compensation aside, *the least they are due is an apology. That's just what the External Affairs Department led us to believe Canada had received in the patients' name.* Last January, External Affairs Minister Allan MacEachen's office said Canada had received an apology from the U.S. Government. When pressed, however, officials couldn't find anything in writing. They surmised the apology had been given orally. Now, according to John Kind, U.S. officials deny ever making an apology. *"I never expressed regret,"* said Richard Smith, number two at the U.S. Embassy in Ottawa until last year. *"I think the situation is regrettable, but that's different, isn't it? I never expressed any regret on the part of the U.S. Government."* As an American would say, that's swell, Mr. Smith. Pay some crazy doctor to screw up people's minds in a friendly country in aid of crushing communism or whatever, then don't even show the class or decency to apologize 25 years later. How Mr. MacEachen will now square this assertion that the U.S. expressed "deep regret" with Mr. Smith's class act remains to be seen.[25]

As in the previous two cases, an apology, even to a third party, would have confirmed the actions in question in the sense of producing official and incontrovertible truths. As such, it would have provided strong grounds for some form of compensation and the acceptance of blame for the offenses. On the other hand, two questions remain. From whom would the injured parties have received an apology? And what would it have signified? From Dr. Cameron, an instrument of the CIA? From the CIA, an agency of the U.S. government? From the U.S. government itself? Even before the revelation that American officials had not apologized, there was no indication that a direct apology was considered appropriate, but only one to Canada "in the patients'" name. If it were simply a question of assigning legal liability—not a trifling matter in this or the other two examples—it would not make much difference to the victims or their survivors. But as we have seen elsewhere, something else is at stake here with regard to apology. And that is the fact that apology is radically transfigured and distorted where heartfelt remorse and a shared sense of what constitutes humane and decent conduct have been banished or diluted by instrumental imperatives. In the end, this example demonstrates, with unequivocal and immaculate cynicism, a central point that has been stressed repeatedly: if sorrow and regret are at the heart of apology, they must be expressed. It is simply not enough to feel sorry but to say so in order to convert a private condition into public communion.[26]

The Pedagogy of Apology

In the previous sections, I have tried to point out the complications arising from third-party intervention and the ways in which they shift the focus and grounds of apologetic discourse. Before leaving this theme, let us pause to consider a crucial and problematic context in which a third party can play a pivotal role. It is in the process of socialization, or what may be referred to more narrowly and aptly as the pedagogy of apology, that the engaged bystander has an especially privileged position. What I have in mind is the common triadic pattern that is generated when an adult enters into or is invited to adjudicate a conflict between two juniors. It is most likely this configuration in which children and other alleged innocents first become acquainted with the idea of apology and its requirements. Most of us, I think, can recall incidents in which parents, kin, teachers, or other superordinates solicited an apology to a sibling, relative, friend, or neighbor, in the course of which the third party brought pressure to bear, explained, coached, exemplified, cajoled, demanded, and so on.

Such initial and initiatory encounters with the social, psychological, and linguistic intricacies of apologetic discourse provide fertile ground for teaching and learning its rudiments, especially if one or both principals identify with the authority figure. As these moral scripts are enacted time and again, the child is alternatively cast in the roles of apologizer and forgiver. Confining ourselves to the situation in which both the offender and the offended are socially naive and an authoritative member intervenes, let us consider some of the more critical pedagogical dynamics from the perspectives of the participants.[27]

First, the wrongdoer is apprised of the distinction between accountable and unaccountable actions, alerted to the existence of an offense gradient or standard of severity, and admonished for conduct that specifically calls for an expression of remorse in lieu of, or in addition to, other forms of restitution. Second, the transgressor is also instructed and monitored with respect to the techniques and mechanics of apology such as proper wording, tone, demeanor, physical posture, and other meta-communicative nuances. Here, as in other areas of social and moral tuition, the socializing agent is faced with the dual task of eliciting behavioral conformity to norms while inculcating an inner commitment and appropriate emotional response.[28]

In this connection, an adequate performance without the apposite affective display, at least up to a certain age, may be acceptable if it is viewed as a prelude to the ideal merging of the two components. To put it another way, a perspicacious third party can tell when the apology produced under pressure is not genuine, that is, lacks spontaneous feelings of remorse, but trust that the offender's compliance with externals will eventually enable the appropriate sentiments to emerge and take shape.

Third, and perhaps most challenging, to the extent that this kind of moral indoctrination is effective, the victim is taught a complex lesson about anger and apology. Whereas the offender's project calls for the suppression of accounts, the willing relinquishment of whatever advantage was gained by the violation, and the expression of real sorrow, the victim's has to do with nurturing a sense of righteous anger and indignation. It was this, after all, that occasioned the intercession of the third party and prompted the call for an apology.

Symbolically, the third party comes to assume the role of the victim, but with an ethical sophistication the child lacks. With lesser or greater skill, the moral tutor demonstrates and acts out a particular formulation of anger for the benefit of the actual victim that calls for nothing less than an apology. The latter is shown what authorizes righteous anger as opposed to retaliation, tears, submission, fear, placatory efforts, etc., and, more important, how to be angry in the service of forgiveness rather than vindictiveness. The intervener thus emerges as a kind of moral stand-in or surrogate, a necessarily temporary social actor whose success is gauged by the extent to which the understudy, the victim, supplants him or her. The ideal sequence in the relationship between the third party and the victim from the beginning of the episode to its conclusion would involve a complementary set of roles and displacements, with the third party moving from spectator to protagonist to spectator, and the victim from protagonist to spectator to protagonist. At the same time, as the recipient of an apology from the chastened and, let us assume, contrite wrongdoer, the injured party is constrained to close the moral circle by cultivating and exercising the faculty of forgiveness. Finally, repetitions of this model are likely to lay the foundations for more durable moral orientations toward deviance, apology, and forgiveness.

It goes without saying that such projects rarely proceed smoothly and require both committed and energetic third parties with some understanding of what apologetic discourse is all about. For example, among children there are numerous points of potential conflict and resistance to learning subtle interpersonal rules that may be perceived as being abstract, arbitrary, burdensome, and costly. Even when youngsters are amenable, communicative incompetence, inconsistency, or lack of authority can undermine the efforts of adults. Although most members do eventually learn the appropriate behavioral procedures and emotions that apologetic discourse requires, some do not, or only imperfectly. Without necessarily subscribing to either a psychoanalytical or sociological determinism, excluding other influences that mold human character, or implying a direct causal connection, let us briefly consider some possible long-term effects of negative apologetic experience or ineffective intervention in its tuition.

Habitual, persistent, or traumatic violations of one's sense of justice and fairness in the home, playground, classroom, and other childhood habitats may so distort the process as to produce characteristic responses to the call in later life. From the perspective of the putative transgressor, for example, this can come about by being forced to apologize for something one did not do or can account for; from that of the victim, by being pressured to forgive what is deemed unforgivable. Thus one common pattern is the person who has mastered the techniques of apology in order to cope, control, or exploit, but without the concomitant spirit. In triadic interaction, the victim in this situation plays a necessary but minor role in what is essentially a dramatic display by the alleged offender to convince the intervening authority that an apology has indeed been made. In the absence of third parties, and in its more developed form, this kind of individual adaptation presents us with a familiar social type: the congenital or compulsive apologizer whose endless pleadings make a mockery of sorrow and debase forgiveness.

By contrast, another recognizable tendency entails the inability or unwillingness to apologize to another under any circumstances. In this case, moral insensibility, arrogance, anger, fear, uncompromising self-righteousness, etc., independently or in combination, manage to overcome and defeat sorrow and regret. Similarly, some individuals (and groups) find it difficult, if not impossible, to accept an apology no matter how contrite the offender or how great the social disruption caused by the rejection. They prefer, it seems, to nurture their anger, hatred, and sense of betrayal. Instead of forgiving and forgetting, they use an apology as the occasion for escalating conflict.

Although these responses are evident in everyday life, literature provides us with especially striking depictions. For instance, it is precisely the volatile combination of extremes—the refusal or reluctance to give or to accept an apology—that is a guiding and central moral theme in one of the greatest works in all of Western literature. These flaws, among others, mark the characters of Agamemnon and Achilles, foster and sustain the inexorable tension between them, and trigger the destructive and tragic consequences narrated in the *Iliad*.[29] Dostoevsky deals with the same motif in the advice Mitya Karamazov offers to his younger brother, Alyosha, after having treated Grushenka badly when she visited him in prison:

"It just kills me when I think of Grusha, it just kills me. . . . She was here earlier today and. . . ."

"She told me she had come. You made her very miserable today."

"I know. Damn my lousy character! I was jealous. I felt sorry when I kissed her as she was leaving, but I didn't ask her to forgive me."

"Why not?" Alyosha cried in surprise.

Mitya laughed almost gaily.

"You're just a little boy, Alyosha, so here's a piece of advice for you: never ask the woman you love for forgiveness! Especially if you really love her, however guilty you may be before her. A woman is so peculiar, Alyosha. Damn it, that's one subject I really know quite a bit about. I tell you, the moment you admit to a woman that you've wronged her and ask her to forgive you, she'll never stop showering you with reproaches. No woman will ever just forgive you for what you've done. First she'll humiliate you as much as she can and remind you of all the mistakes you've ever made, and even of those you never made; she will forget nothing and add plenty, and only then will she forgive you. And that's how the best, the nicest of them, act! She'll scrape the bottom of the barrel and pour it over your head—it's an instinct in those angels, without whom we cannot live. You see, Alyosha, my boy, I'll tell you frankly—every self-respecting man is bound to land under the heel of some woman at one time or another. That's my conviction, or rather a feeling I have. A man should be forgiving—it will never degrade him. Forgiving will not stain even a hero, not even Caesar! And yet you must never ask a woman to forgive you—anything rather than that! I want you to remember this rule, taught you by your older brother Mitya, who perished because of women. No, I think I'd better make it up to Grusha in some other way, without asking her to forgive me."[30]

The ultimate negatory stance in a culture that does accord a place for apology would be the categorical denial of any obligation to respond to the call or, for that matter, even to give an account for an offense. This quintessentially amoral position is succinctly expressed in the dictum "never apologize, never explain." To which, if taken seriously, it would follow, "never be sorry, never express remorse, never seek forgiveness."[31]

4. *Modes of Apology (2)*

Having considered the moral dialectic of interpersonal apology (the tension between sorrow and forgiveness that is transcended by reconciliation) and the role of third parties, in this chapter I shall focus on the other forms of this discourse.

Apology from the One to the Many

In this case, an individual is faced with the prospect of responding to a call for an apology from a *collective* counterpart or offended other, for example, a group, organization, social category, public, or nebulous aggregate for an alleged violation or infraction.[1] While retaining its basic identity with the more intimate discourse that typically obtains between individuals, no matter how stylized or formal the interaction, this form of apology has an underlying dynamic that gives it a unique stamp. Its distinction, I shall try and show, derives primarily from the condition of plurality: the presence and mobilization of an offended Many. Let us begin, therefore, by delving into some of the more important contingencies and constraints introduced by this structural factor.

In the first place, the transgressor is subject to increased exposure and vulnerability. If, as suggested earlier, we stand naked and defenseless under the moral gaze of the *one* we have wronged, multiple scrutiny and reproach can be all the more excoriating, unsettling, and humbling. This is especially so when the violation places one's own membership (or even life) in jeopardy, but is also something non-members have to contend with in their dealings with collectivities.[2]

Plurality, in this confrontation between One and Many, does more, however, than simply intensify the sense of intimidation or dread and increase the social visibility of the individual offender. In addition, it allows for a kind of collective surveillance and monitoring that is only partially realizable at the interpersonal level. Practically speaking, we can more easily (if so inclined) remain out of earshot of a call emanating from a single voice than remain deaf to a chorus of accusers (and potential redeemers) acting in concert.

But this, too, is not all that can be effected by sheer numbers or the bearers of a shared grievance. Excepting the most energetic, dedicated, and tenacious of individuals, the Many enjoy the advantage of corporate continuity, of being able to persist in their efforts to obtain satisfaction and, through a similar enduring capacity inherent in plurality, to keep the memory of the violation alive over time.[3]

The final and, in many respects, most important difference between this configuration and interpersonal apology has to do with the related issues of privacy and publicity. We have already suggested (in our discussion of third parties) how a movement from the private to the public realm radically alters the grounds of interaction and bargaining positions of the principals and imposes constraints upon their flexibility. What should be stressed in this connection is that while the potentiality for such a shift in discursive space is always present in One to One apology, it nevertheless remains no more than a possibility or contingency.

By contrast, apologetic discourse between the One and the Many takes place and unfolds in a public domain from beginning to end, no matter how limited the engaged public may be. It is this that invests the exchange with new purpose and significance. For publicity, ventilated speech, does more than direct attention to a plurality of offended parties; it situates the offender in a sociolinguistic territory whose logic and economy require a particular kind of display or, more aptly, performance.[4] For example, the personal, pragmatic, and cloistered dialogue between individuals allows for, if not secures, considerable leeway and mutual adjustments not only with respect to reaching a satisfactory resolution of difference but also in terms of the expressive style employed. In other words, once the offender has indicated a genuine sense of sorrow, its mode of expression or "saying" becomes a necessary but subordinate locutionary exercise whose success is virtually assured. The sorrow, that is, takes precedence over the speech, which, depending on the offender's rhetorical skills, may range from the laconic to the elaborately eloquent. When the call comes from a collectivity, however, there is a subtle but telling change in emphasis and execution. Here the offender is summoned into a world of records, social bookkeeping, and punctiliousness in which the speech act itself, *qua* performance, becomes paramount. And in such a world, everything counting as the apology must be spelled out; nothing can be taken for granted or remain ambiguous. Thus the energies of the One are invested in display, and the overriding interest of the Many is to put the apology "on record," that is, to extract a public, chronicled recantation that restores those aspects of the collectivity's integrity and honor called into question by the offense.

In order to conform to this agenda, which necessarily entails representation of the collectivity's moral position in a wider social order, the transgressor is obliged to produce, as it were, "on record" speech. This, in turn, requires a species of solemn, incantational language—an official utterance closely akin to written discourse that is, by and large, alien to the vital, ephemeral, and allusive speech characteristic of even the most estranged intimates. As a consequence, there is a displacement and reordering of priorities with respect to the dynamic composite of emotion and its articulation. Specifically, in the interpersonal realm, sorrow is central and its expression is derivative. The reverse seems to be the case in the public sphere; sorrow gives way, is overshadowed and subverted by the apparent compulsion to generate unambiguous speech. Because the whole discourse is filtered and channeled through this collective need to have it on the record, the apology is transformed into a type of socially validated testimony, and the offender into a kind of witness.

Within a broader perspective, to digress briefly, this type of apologetic discourse is but one remedial or retributive strategy, among others, for dealing with individuals who are viewed as threats to the legitimacy and claims of collective representations. The image of the One giving testimony, bearing witness before the Many (or its personification), is a familiar, recurrent, and powerful one in human history. Dramatic examples are not hard to come by: Jesus' encounters with the Pharisees and Pilate, public confessions, inquisitions, martyrdoms, the trials of Socrates and Dreyfus, the Stalinist purges, the McCarthy hearings, and Maoist rehabilitations. In literature, there is Orwell's *1984*; in art, *The Woman Taken in Adultery*, as depicted by both Rembrandt and William Blake. What is common to all of these is the theme of the One in opposition to the Many, with the outcome—depending upon the perceived stakes and resources of the parties—being reconciliation, probation, exclusion, or death.[5]

Although this form of apology is relatively less conspicuous in Western societies than in cultures in which honor is stressed, conformity valued, and individuality suppressed, such as in Japan or other settings in which political or religious orthodoxy is strictly enforced, it is by no means unknown or inconsequential. Although Nixon's case stands out as a particularly notorious and momentous occasion, the fact that less celebrated incidents are considered newsworthy by the media indicates that this form of apology is not extinct and probably more widespread than we would suspect or predict on purely theoretical grounds.

More to the point, apologies of this type figure in a variety of situations in which legal or quasi-legal corporate sanctions are inapplicable, inadequate, premonitory, or play a subsidiary role in dealing with transgressions by individuals. Subject as they are to the conditions of plurality previously noted, they involve precarious and transcendent communicative acts in which public contrition and symbolic restitution by the individual constitute the means of restoring the collectivity to its state of purity while rehabilitating the transgressor. It is precisely these considerations that take precedence over material compensation, juridical penalties, or other reparative measures.[6] More often than not, the violation pales in significance as collective attention focuses on receptiveness to the call as the pivotal criterion for judging the offender's character and fate.

Consider, in this context, two telling instances from academia:

It's been years since anyone took Bob Hope seriously and the 76-year-old comedian must have been surprised when officials of the University of Florida demanded he apologize for remarks he made about their school. He was at the Gator Bowl, a kind of homecoming party and variety show, doing his usual geographical put-down: "Here I am at the University of Florida where going to class is an extra-curricular activity." The serious-minded in the crowd were not amused. There was even an editorial in The Independent Florida Alligator which went on about the university's "ranked programs, nationally known faculty members, and academic awards." Hope threw in the towel and his press agent issued an apology: "Bob Hope's humor is intended to distract or nudge, but not penetrate," the statement read. "If someone takes offense, apologies are in order, that's his personal feeling."[7]

And on an equally sensitive issue, we are informed:

The chancellor of the University of Missouri–Kansas City in Kansas City has issued his second apology in a month for a joke he made about rape. "Once again, I want to express my apologies to anyone offended by remarks I made," chancellor George Russell said in a statement. "They were inappropriate and insensitive and I regret I made them." Russell, opening a Women in Public Leadership Seminar, told the group about an intruder who came to a house and was asked if he was a burglar. When the intruder replied he was a rapist, the story continued, the resident said he would call his wife. He is the second official in the university system to become embroiled in a controversy stemming from comments about rape. Robert Dempster of Sikeston, a university curator—equivalent to a trustee—apologized earlier this fall for a remark he made about rape at a meeting in July.[8]

Of the many anecdotes and examples culled from various sources, two serve particularly well on a number of counts as "clarifying depictions" of apology from the One to the Many.[9] First, they are relatively unambiguous in the sense that an apology (or refusal to apologize) is a major point of contention. Second, in both cases, the offender's group membership is at stake or called into question. Finally, despite their differing circumstances and institutional settings, they reveal certain structural similarities that explicate the character of this kind of discourse and that recur, with more or less clarity, in other contexts. In other terms, here, as throughout, my formulations do not, I submit, depend upon the timeliness of my examples.

The first exemplar concerns an incident (unlikely to be known or remembered by anyone except an absolute aficionado) involving a major-league baseball player who was forced to apologize publicly for behavior off the field that, as it turned out, was not legally actionable. An account of the details and unfolding of this elaborate social production was reported in the press as follows:

Admitting he had been "in the wrong place at the wrong time doing the wrong thing," Cleon Jones accepted yesterday a record $2000 fine by the [New York] Mets and a tongue-lashing from the club's chairman, M. Donald Grant.

In a bizarre setting in Shea Stadium's news room, the left fielder stood next to his wife, Angela, while Grant said he had soiled the Mets' image "of having clean ballplayers."

A few hours earlier, charges against Jones for indecent exposure had been dropped by the state attorney's office in St. Petersburg, Fla. Jones was arrested there on May 4 at 5:30 A.M., when the police said they had found him asleep in the nude in a van with Sharon Ann Sabol, 21 years old, who described herself as an unemployed waitress.

Miss Sabol, from Johnson City, N.Y., also was charged with possessing narcotics (the police said a marijuana cigarette had been found in her purse) and "narcotic implements."

The state attorney, James T. Russell, said by telephone from Clearwater, Fla., yesterday that she had been given immunity and the charges against her dropped. He would not say why she had received immunity.

Meanwhile, Baseball Commissioner Bowie Kuhn's office also closed its investigation of Jones. Although Jones was not charged with possession of or use of marijuana, Kuhn sent his chief of security, Henry Fitzgibbon, to determine whether the player was involved with drugs in Florida.

Grant bristled when asked what right the club had to fine Jones when according to law-enforcement authorities, no crime had been committed.

"It was bad for baseball's image," he snapped.

"It was in the newspapers."

Jones signed a statement saying: "I wish to apologize publicly to my wife and children, the Mets' ownership and management, my teammates, to all

Met fans and to baseball in general for my behavior in St. Petersburg."

His future with the team appeared clouded.

Jones, 32 years old, underwent cartilage surgery on his left knee last October. He has been on the disabled list since and in Florida, still bound by the team's training rules, he was attempting to work himself into shape. . . .

Mrs. Jones listened impassively while Grant recounted her husband's misdeeds. Then she said, "I believe Cleon. I trust him. We've been married 11 years and I've known him 15 years."

Jones said it would take "a few days to right myself" in the field, and added "I'm ready mentally." He said it was important to him that fans and teammates realized "I'm not a bad guy."

There appeared to be some confusion why Jones had been arrested. A police source who worked on the case said the charges against him had been dropped because "someone has to be exposed to the indecency to make the charge stick." No residents had complained to the police.

The arresting officers contended that Jones and Miss Sabol were in a station wagon "with the windows rolled down." Presumably, they would have been seen easily. However, the police said yesterday that the vehicle was a "side-loading van."[10]

The next day, this story appeared in the same newspaper:

The head of the Major League Baseball Players Association accused the Mets yesterday of "a tasteless display of economic power," and of seeking to humiliate Cleon Jones. Marvin Miller made the charges after the Mets fined Jones $2,000 and made him read a public apology for his arrest on indecent exposure charges in St. Petersburg, Fla. "There's nothing I can do," said Miller. He explained that only a player can initiate an appeal on a fine.

Jones did not appeal. After further problems with the club and several unsuccessful attempts by the Mets to trade him, he requested and received his unconditional release on 27 July 1975. Cleon Jones ended his thirteen-year major-league career with the Chicago White Sox in 1976, playing in only twelve games.

Let us begin our analysis of this case with some obvious but not thereby insignificant observations on the text. In the second paragraph, our eyewitness correspondent describes the setting and, it may be concluded from the tone of what follows, the proceedings as "bizarre." This word is commonly understood to mean something (or someone) extraordinary, strikingly unconventional, out of place, odd, or eccentric. In this instance, it is applied to a situation in which a member of an organization is publicly castigated, fined, and forced to participate in a staged piacular rite. Now taken as a paradigm of penalization, this is hardly unusual and occurs routinely in homes, schools, and, perhaps in its fullest elaboration, courts of law. Could it be said, then, that this usage (and judgment) is merely an expression of bias on the part of a tendentious outsider? I think not. Confining ourselves to this particular occasion, I would submit that this designation is an accurate description that hinges on two essential and interrelated considerations central to the dynamics of apologetic discourse between the One and the Many. The first of these concerns the distinction between "official" and actual scripts and strategies. The second has to do with the crucial role of third parties in endorsing the moral claims and charges put forth by any collectivity. Moreover, as will become evident, this account provides us with an instructive example of an abortive morality play, a flawed "degradation ceremony" that, while failing to achieve its desired goal, nevertheless manages to degrade.[11] These comments call for amplification.

The elements and interlinkages that combined to generate an opposing, but parallel, testimony that effectively subverted official definitions and desires may be understood as answers to questions about the network of categories pertaining to apology that radically transformed the discursive context. To see how this came about, and why the situation struck the reporter (and others) as "bizarre," obliges us to recast the published account in terms of these categories and their shifting meanings.

The genesis of the discrepancy between the intended purpose of the denunciation and the results effected may be charted as follows. The express plan of the presiders, represented by Grant as spokesman for the collectivity, called for an apology from Jones to those he had supposedly offended by his conduct before witnesses in a public forum. The stated grounds of Jones's social and moral demotion, together with the means for his return to institutional grace, appeared straightforward, if stringent. Everything seemed in order: an offense, an offender, offended parties, the apology, and witnesses to record the details of the condemnation and reconciliation. But Grant and the Mets seriously miscalculated. Their scheduled scenario and script missed the mark by a wide margin and lacked verisimilitude on a number of grounds.

In the first place, the exact nature of Jones's transgression was never unequivocally stated by the Mets. Apart from the fact that Jones had broken the team's training rules—a common enough occurrence that could easily have been dealt with internally—the ostensible offense, and avowed justification for holding the press conference, was his arrest on charges of indecent exposure. But as the Mets knew, these charges had been dismissed before the interested parties convened. Furthermore, there was no evidence that Jones had been involved with narcotics. Despite these developments, they proceeded, which strongly suggests that something else was at stake. In effect, then, Jones was being heavily fined, publicly humiliated, and forced by his employers to apologize for conduct that was not subject to legal penalty. The rancorous and surrealistic atmosphere of the gathering was exacerbated when Grant was queried about this apparent anomaly. Reiterating the gist of his opening remarks, he testily passed over this inconsistency by invoking the authority of extra-legal professional and ethical standards as grounds for his denunciation. According to this view, the deeper import of Jones's actions did not reside within the narrow compass of the law but in broader issues related to corporate prestige and repute. From this premise it followed that although Jones had not violated the law, he was still accountable to the club and fans for what he had done. In this context, the metaphors of "image" and "reflection," negatively couched in terms of profanation and disgrace, were at the heart of Grant's diatribe and discourse. After all was said and done, he maintained, Jones had soiled the Mets' image "of having clean ballplayers;" the incident was "bad for baseball's image. It was in the newspapers."

This tack—whether it was part of the official script or impromptu is immaterial—not only served to supersede legal criteria of innocence and guilt but, through its pejorative allusiveness, to enlarge the scope of culpability. Thus it implied that what Jones had done was more than an isolated impropriety; it was the issue and mark of his basal character or "total identity." [12] The efficacy of this attribution was affirmed by Jones's poignant *personal* statement concerning the importance of having the fans and his teammates recognize that "I'm not a bad guy," and his wife's testimonial, "I believe in Cleon. I trust him." As the text and other evidence demonstrate, however, Grant's approach was ultimately self-defeating. In his zeal to salvage an initially dubious project that was rapidly turning into a debacle, he ended up in a classic double-bind situation: in the process of challenging Jones's moral integrity, he alienated those whose assent was necessary for a successful denunciation.[13]

How did this come about and contribute to the perceived bizarreness of this public spectacle? At the risk of taxing the reader's patience, let us recount a few points that are crucial to our interpretation. If it was plain that no crime had been committed, this is not to say that no wrong had been done. As Jones himself candidly (and apparently under no duress) admitted, he had been "in the wrong place at the wrong time doing the wrong thing." In addition to being a professional athlete and member of the Mets organization, he was married. Now except in the most permissive social circles, it is axiomatic in North American culture that married persons are expected to lie naked in beds, vans, or elsewhere for that matter, only with their spouses. Jones was apprehended in compromising circumstances with a woman other than his wife. Such conjugal indiscretions, especially on the part of those inhabiting domains that, whatever their realities, are still considered sacrosanct, for example, sports, typically provide fodder for various media and divorce suits as well as causing interpersonal strife. But, and this is the nub of the matter, they are only rarely defined as occasions for public censure of the kind Jones suffered at the hands of his superiors in the presence of the one he had truly hurt.[14]

Thus, once formal grounds for the punishment and demotion disappeared, the Mets were placed on the defensive and had to come up with an alternative rationale to justify the proceedings. They not only failed in their efforts but revealed that the case they were trying to build against Jones was really predicated on anger and vindictiveness. Two injustices had been committed. First, the punishment was gratuitous and harsh. Second, the forum of denunciation was inappropriate. As a consequence, Jones's status as an offender was only remotely connected with what the organization claimed. As far as witnesses at the event (and others) were concerned, his particular offense was not within the purview or jurisdiction of the collectivity. Rather than being the object of public scrutiny, it more decorously warranted private travail. Contrary to what the Mets had planned, staged, and hoped for, the sympathies of the witnesses devolved upon Jones, while Grant and the management emerged as mean-spirited, self-serving, and sanctimonious bullies.

There is something else that should be noted here. Ruled as they are by context and convention, all speech acts, no matter how blunt or finely honed by veiled intentions, are subject to semantic inversion, that is, the reception and imposition of disparate or antithetical meanings. In this instance, official representations were subverted by a sort of discursive drift, so to speak, that culminated in an interesting set of categorical substitutions. For example, at the outset, Jones was the designated offender charged with damaging the image of the Mets and baseball for having been arrested, though not arraigned, for the unsavory act of indecent exposure. By the time the proceedings were concluded, however, Grant and the Mets had displaced him as offenders for having presided over a kangaroo court and publicly abusing a helpless and vulnerable employee. Jones's transgression, contrary to the Mets' contentions, was not conceived as a grave threat to their moral order but rather as an exemplification of perhaps the most common, comprehensible, and in this case, at least, forgivable of human failings—"being in the wrong place at the wrong time doing the wrong thing."

A similar disjunction between official pronouncements and their reception may be discerned with respect to the apology itself and the role of witnesses. These disparities and transformations unfolded in such a manner as to produce two versions of apology, on the one hand, and strategic defections, on the other. These patterns merit close scrutiny.

Our text informs us that Jones signed and read the following statement: "I wish to apologize publicly to my wife and children, the Mets' ownership and management, my teammates, to all Met fans and to baseball in general for my behavior in St. Petersburg."

Although we have no conclusive evidence, the inclusive, sweeping nature and wording of the apology (ranging from intimates to "baseball in general"), together with Grant's comments, strongly suggest that Jones was not its author. Moreover, following the Mets' lead, the apology contains no specification of the offense in question apart from the vague reference to "my behavior in St. Petersburg." These deficiencies notwithstanding, Jones played his assigned role and, in a sense, confirmed what Grant and the Mets had promulgated and sought to establish. But this concession could not, alone, bear the burden of the discourse. While such agreement or identity is something that every call for a public apology seeks to achieve and record, it does so at the risk of severing its vital connection with sorrow. That is, one may, for many reasons, conform to the demands of the Many without thereby undergoing alteration of the moral sensibility a genuine apology requires. And this was the most glaring of all the defects thus far noted in the formal apology. Bound to a narrow logic that could accommodate only its own premises and purposes, placing its reliance on self-evidence, allusion, and the presumption of shared moral indignation, the purported apology contained only those elements the collectivity deemed essential to its cause, that is, an offender, an ambiguous offense, and a list of officially designated and supposedly offended parties. Finally, to underscore its intent, the term "apology" was used. But conspicuously missing in the declaration was something only Jones could provide—*sorrow and regret*. All of these factors thus conspired to deprive the official apology of any moral force it laid claim to, exposing its coercive and spurious nature.

If the authorized apology lacked any semblance of credibility, the authentic version surfaced in Jones's terse but telling assertion that "it was important to him that fans and teammates realized 'I'm not a bad guy.'" In these few spontaneous words, Jones nicely summarized the moral nuances that had eluded Grant and turned the tide of popular sentiment against the Mets. His statement not only acknowledged his wrongdoing and denied the Mets' negative attributions concerning his total identity but also indicated contrition. In effect, and the reader may judge the soundness of this formulation by consulting the text itself, Jones was saying: "I'm not what the Mets make me out to be. As a husband, father, member of the team, and professional athlete, I have certain obligations. What I did, whether illegal or not, was wrong. What people think of me matters. What I did was bad, but I'm not a bad guy. I'm sorry." Nothing like this, in either the reported or paraphrased version, came close to being expressed in the apology of record.

We come, finally, to the eyewitnesses. At various places, Garfinkel reminds us of their strategic function in degradation ceremonies. For example, "To be successful, the denunciation must redefine the situation of those that are witnesses to the denunciation work."[15] And, "What the denouncer says must be regarded by the witnesses as true on the grounds of a socially employed metaphysics whereby witnesses assume that witnesses and denouncer are alike in essence."[16] From the denouncer's point of view, it follows, witnesses inhabit an unstable social space between neutrality and potential partisanship or opposition. Consequently, they must be courted, swayed, moved to identify with the denouncer, and ultimately convinced that the censure is condign and that the social demotion of the accused is just and necessary. While this is a delicate enough rhetorical achievement under favorable conditions, it becomes all the more formidable when witnesses are non-members and thus relatively immune to collective sanctions, that is, without fear of reprisal or hope of reward. In such a situation, the goal of the denouncer is to convert initial disinterest or mere curiosity into active support and endorsement by cultivating a sense of shared interests and treating the witnesses as quasi-members.[17] As it turned out, however, Grant and the Mets not only failed to rally the witnesses but irreparably alienated them through a series of cumulative blunders. Let us see how this came about.

The decision to hold a press conference instead of simply issuing a news release announcing Jones's fine turned the initial dyadic pattern of interaction into a triadic one, activated the heretofore dormant social category of witness, and put the Mets, as well as Jones, on public display. Once they accepted the invitation to the formal assembly, the reporter-witnesses found themselves in an ambiguous and difficult position. Ostensibly, their job was to render an accurate account of the event for their readers. To second the Mets' claims and join in the denunciation would not only have violated professional standards but also have revealed them as hacks and lackeys. It is hard to imagine that the Mets realistically expected such unqualified, uncritical support from hardened New York sports writers and others. So what, then, was their role insofar as the collectivity was concerned? Essentially, their usefulness to the Mets resided in their capacity as impartial recorders and, so to speak, heralds. But this was not to be because, unlike the ideal messenger, they were active participants in producing and authenticating the message. In other words, the journalists emerged as interlocutors rather than passive auditors or scribes.

As we have also seen, they eventually defined their role as witnesses in adversative terms. A thorny issue from the start was the fit between punishment and offense, which was aggravated by Grant's angry reply when he was challenged to justify his stand. This exchange underscored the fundamental discord between the denouncer and witnesses and raised other points of contention about their choice of the discursive arena, authorship of the apology, the presence of Jones's wife, intimidation, and related matters.

Most damaging of all, however, was the coalescence of these negative cadences into a disquieting sense of personal contamination on the part of the witnesses. After all was said and done, no expression of moral indignation or revulsion, no attempt to distance themselves, could alter the fact that they were physically present and, willynilly, implicated in the symbolic violence being perpetrated against Jones by the Many. It was clear that their attendance was essential to the denunciatory project and justified it, even though they did not include themselves among the presumed offended parties but sided with Jones. When it became evident that they had been co-opted, they withdrew their allegiance to what Grant needed most—credibility. Indeed, the credibility of the whole spectacle, not merely specific points, was called into question and ultimately came to be defined as bizarre, unbelievable, and obscene. Not, however, before the degradation they were witnessing and legitimating spilled over and soiled them. As one prominent writer and keen student of baseball responded when queried about this case:

I'm afraid I can't help much with your request for information about that Cleon Jones incident. I didn't attend the press conference at which Cleon was forced to abase himself, so I have no notes that would tell me just when it took place. Friends who were there told me later that it was one of the most degrading and embarrassing events they had ever attended; I mean, it degraded everybody, including the reporters.[18]

One final irony should be noted. If the witnesses could not avoid defilement, the published account, however brief, served to avenge or redeem them insofar as it provided readers with an alternative and competing historical record of what had occurred. It accomplished this not only by discrediting Grant and the Mets but by bringing attention to the fact that a discourse other than the official one was being carried on that could neither be ignored nor covered up.

Our second example of the One to Many form is somewhat less convoluted in that it hinges more directly upon the issue of apology and involves third parties only peripherally. The details are as follows:

Carlisle, Pa. (AP)—After six years, Robert Bear still insists he will not take the easy way back into his family's affections—apologizing to the Reformed Mennonite Church.

Bear was excommunicated in 1972 and has been shunned since then by the rest of the congregation, including his wife and six children.

His family was ordered by the church not to talk to him, except when necessary, and his wife, Gale, was told to stop being his mate. That was the hardest part, Bear, 49, said in an interview.

The family lives separately. Bear moved out of his farmhouse to a trailer; his wife and children live about 30 kilometres away.

When they were still living under the same roof, his children sometimes called him "sick," or worse, during arguments over his religious beliefs. His oldest son David, 17, once tried to run him over with a tractor in a fit of anger, Bear said.

Bear says he will keep trying for reconciliation, despite repeated failure. He sued the church in court for alienation of his wife's affections. He lost.

Periodically, he tries to bring his family to live with him in his trailer. Once, he recalls, his daughter Rachel, 12, cursed at him when he went for a visit.

"I said, 'Well that's enough' and put her in the car and took her home." Within hours police arrived and Bear landed in a psychiatric hospital for three days observation.

Bear says he will never accept the church's offer to take him back if he repents. "I'll never be a Reformed Mennonite again, but I intend to get my wife and children straightened around. That's what keeps me going."

He puts in long days growing crops on his 300-acre farm here but his energy goes into his one-man war with a church he says is "playing God."

The Reformed Mennonite Church, with headquarters in Lancaster, Pa., is a branch of the fundamentalist Mennonite faith. It teaches that people who criticize church practices are guilty of "raillery" and must be excommunicated—or "shunned."

Bear's misdeed: he questioned why his mother-in-law and her husband were given communion despite the widespread knowledge that they were separated. He says communion is normally denied in such situations.

The "shunning" is loosely enforced, Bear said, and at times his wife would talk to him. At other times, he said, she would stare him down like the disbelieving heretic her church had branded him.

Mrs. Bear's brother, Bishop Glenn Gross, now heads Bear's former 25-member congregation. It was Gross, says Bear, who engineered his ouster. Gross no longer discusses the matter with reporters, saying the dispute was treated unfairly by the media in the past.[19]

In order to bring into sharper focus the tensions and complexities inherent in apologetic discourse between the One and the Many, let us reconstruct the details of this conflict in its various stages.

Stage 1. The domestic and religious *status quo ante bellum*, as it were, found Bear, his wife, and children living together and members in good standing of the church. Bear's mother-in-law and her husband were separated but, as may be inferred from the published account, also members of the Reformed Mennonite Church. His wife's brother, Gross, was an influential member of the church and at the time of the news report was a bishop and head of the congregation. From the information at hand, it is impossible to ascertain the nature of kin relations or strains during this period.

Stage 2. The source of conflict and what precipitated the disagreement was Bear's questioning of the church's authority to give communion to members who were married but separated, specifically with regard to his mother-in-law and her husband. At this point, the budding feud was confined to the relatively private spheres of family and congregation, with the pertinent relationships presumably intact, if contentious. As yet, there was no identifiable transgression.

Stage 3. Bear's status as a deviant and offender was officially proclaimed when church leaders defined his protest and challenge to their authority as heretical. He was charged with "raillery," that is, criticizing church practices, and the punishment imposed was a form of exclusion until such time as he formally apologized and repented. For all practical and social purposes, his membership was suspended. Bear claimed that Gross was responsible for this course of action.

Stage 4. The discord between Bear and the collectivity escalated because the "shunning" was not limited to church-related activities but extended to his immediate family and included a ban on conjugal relations. By this time, the offender's differences with the ecclesiastical authorities widened beyond the initial disagreement and served as a catalyst for family violence and estrangement. We have now moved to a situation in which the offense, the offender, and offended have been identified, a penalty imposed, and a call for an apology laid down as the sole means of reconciliation.

Stage 5. This was a crucial phase because it signaled an impasse and transformed the disagreement into a full-blown public dispute.[20] Bear sued the church for alienation of his wife's affections and lost. Following an argument with one of his children, which led the police and psychiatrists to intervene, he was placed under observation for three days. Bear was now living alone; his dispute with the church and his family had received considerable and sympathetic media coverage. The conflict was now fully in the public domain.

Stage 6. At the time the story appeared, the disputants remained far apart, their positions had hardened, and the prospects for any kind of reconciliation appeared dim. The church remained adamant in demanding a public apology as the condition for Bear's reinstatement as a member in good standing and as a sign of repentance. This was also the consideration for a reunion with his family. He, on the other hand, steadfastly refused to apologize and rejected the possibility of renewing his affiliation with the church, although he still had hopes of effecting a reconciliation with his wife and children.

Beyond the factors that made this dispute an eminently newsworthy story—its acrimony, prolonged duration, and divisiveness—

it is of interest to us for two reasons. First, everything ultimately hinged upon a formal apology; and second, it raises the question of the timing of an apology—something we have dealt with only allusively heretofore. Although the two matters are closely bound together empirically, for analytical purposes we shall consider them separately.

Here is a situation in which a man's most intimate and significant bonds, to his family and God, are squarely contingent upon an apology. Bear's life has been totally disrupted because, as his own logic dictates, he will not "take the easy way back" and repent. The question immediately arises as to the kind of speech the Many are demanding as a requirement for wiping the slate clean. Ideally, it would express a radical and heartfelt sense of contrition, acknowledgment of collective righteousness, and a subsequent return to the spiritual and domestic fold. But from the inception of the disagreement it was clear that this was not to be. Bear's persistent and principled dissent, the protracted nature of the dispute, and the strains generated by a clash of loyalties all combined to preclude any mutually satisfying reconciliation. The gulf between the parties was further widened by Bear's appeal to civil authorities for relief (that could not conceivably relieve, given the circumstances) and his brief incarceration. Despite these accumulated grievances and complications, an apology continued to be defined as the only acceptable solution to the quarrel, short of breaking off relations entirely. But what, it may be asked, could it possibly signify at this stage of the conflict? At best, I would argue, little more than what the church wanted at the outset in order to set its house in order: evidence of symbolic and practical capitulation couched in official speech fashioned to reaffirm institutional legitimacy and authority. In other words, a purely formal declaration or recantation in the service of moral and social restitution with little or no concern for authentic sorrow.

Although matters were further complicated when Bear's plight came to the attention of the press, the ensuing publicity, unlike that in the Jones case, did not alter the essential features of the controversy but rather served to accentuate them. Thus, aside from temporarily enlarging the public scope of the conflict, the sporadic intervention of the media placed the church on the defensive, gave voice to the disputants' anger and frustration, and generally contributed to the prevailing indurative atmosphere. Finally, the concept of apology as the indispensable medium of pacification and conciliation, already vitiated and reduced to an arid technicality, now appeared in the catchy headlines of newspapers as little more than a travesty of a just resolution. The inevitable loss of journalistic interest in the proceedings, evident in the absence of a follow-up, signaled not the end of the story but its return to the private sphere in which the principal characters presumably would continue their struggle over the heavy moral freight borne by something as seemingly innocuous and "easy" as an apology.

The Timing of Apology

This example also raises, albeit in an extreme fashion, a delicate problem germane to all forms of apology. This has to do with the temporal dimension of the apologetic process. More specifically, it concerns what are deemed appropriate intervals between the various phases following the identification of an offense. In this regard, a detailed and comprehensive analysis of any concrete sequence would require information on the severity of the offense, the relative and absolute time spans separating the offense, the call for an apology, the offender's response, the victim's reaction, and the outcome. Finally, it should also be possible, within reasonable limits, to distinguish phases even when they overlap to some extent or another. I shall not attempt to trace all these complexities here—the topic merits a study of its own—but rather use the previous example in order to speculate upon the more limited but nevertheless crucial question of the temporal location of the apology itself in relation to the call and forgiveness.

Let me begin by noting that there is a critical, if variable, period following a transgression after which the potential efficacy of an apology diminishes or is nullified. I have in mind here something akin to what the ancient Greeks termed *kairos*, a time when conditions are right or propitious for the accomplishment of an important act or undertaking. Needless to say, precisely what constitutes the auspicious or opportune time may vary from case to case and according to local conditions and definitions. Be that as it may—and this is hardly a novel formulation, but a strategic one for our purposes—the ultimate significance of duration in this context lies in its structural rather than its chronological implications insofar as something of import to the actors (principals or third parties) either does or does not occur within the relevant discursive period. To put it another way, I conceive of duration not in strictly temporal terms but essentially as bracketing a particular discursive space in such a way as to facilitate or constrain certain speech acts. Thus the temporality of duration in apologetic discourse is structural: the "something of import" referred to above is not the passage of time per se, but the nature of discourse and action that takes place in that time period. From this perspective, we can initially identify two normatively deviant configurations or dynamics, potential in any form of sociality but especially pertinent to restorative projects, whereby an apology would be reckoned as coming "too early, quickly, or easily," on the one hand, or "too late," on the other.[21] What are some of the considerations that might lead to such conventional assessments?

If, as suggested throughout, one of the essential functions of an apology is to retrace the offense and convert it into an occasion for sorrow, expiation, and forgiveness, then it cannot fully accomplish its work if it is offered too early or too late.[22] If it precedes or follows too closely upon the heels of a call, it may easily or reasonably be construed as self-serving, a hollow courtesy, or merely a sign of patronizing indifference. Correlatively, personal experience and a variety of descriptions from daily life suggest that the longer one waits following a call, the more difficult it is to apologize, the more carefully one's words must be chosen, and the less the apology is worth. In both instances, failure is the residue of an inability or unwillingness to take cognizance of the *kairos* between the call for an apology and its proffering. In short, there is, so to speak, a tender moment following an offense which, if hastily foreshortened or heedlessly prolonged, is likely to harden hearts rather than allow for a salutary stirring of sorrow and forgiveness.

Even though the call for an apology went unheeded in Bear's case, it is instructive in its own right because it illuminates the socio-dynamics of duration and vividly exemplifies the concept of a discursive period. What was telling here was not the length of time as such, but the collection of injustices and accumulation of recriminations by the parties in the wake of the original falling out. From Bear's point of view, these included social and physical isolation from his family and religious community, an attempted assault by his son, an unsuccessful court action, and the incident with his daughter that led to his brush with police and psychiatrists. Church officials, on the other hand, considered the dispute an internal matter and believed that their position was canonically and morally correct. According to them, Bear was at fault and the whole affair had been treated unfairly and sensationally by the media. This is all familiar ground by now, and it is not our place to judge the merits and claims of either side. What is relevant to our discussion is that the sum total of these derivative actions and reactions conspired to create an inimical atmosphere that grew progressively worse over time. Duration, in other words, did not assuage wounds but rather opened up new ones that, if we may surmise, even apology could not heal.

If we have dealt excessively with the coercive and intimidating aspects of apology from the One to the Many in this section, it would be a mistake to imply that these and related themes completely rule this form of discourse. While it is true, for reasons already cited, that an individual typically experiences external pressures when encountering an offended collectivity, there are also times when these are generated internally by an ethical sensibility in search of relief and release from a singular burden. The unsuccessful attempt of the American who dropped an atomic bomb on Nagasaki to apologize to its citizens forty years later (see note 2) is but one of many cases in point. But the power and poignancy of an internal call for an apology and expression of deep sorrow are perhaps best captured in the following excerpt from a novel about postwar Japan:

He wasn't a bad man. He was just someone who worked very hard doing what he thought was for the best. But you see, Ichiro, when the war ended, things were very different. The songs Mr. Naguchi composed had become very famous, not just in this city, but all over Japan. They were sung on the radio and in bars. And the likes of your Uncle Kenji sang them when they were marching or before battle. And after the war, Mr. Naguchi thought his songs had been—well—a sort of mistake. He thought of all the people who had been killed, all the little boys your age, Ichiro, who no longer had parents, he thought of all these things and he thought perhaps his songs were a mistake. And he felt he should apologize. To everyone who was left. To little boys who no longer had parents. And to parents who had lost little boys like you. To all these people, he wanted to say sorry. I think that's why he killed himself. Mr. Naguchi wasn't a bad man at all, Ichiro. He was brave to admit the mistake he'd made. He was very brave and honourable.[23]

Apology from the Many to the One

When we turn to apology from the Many to the One, we find ourselves in yet another discursive terrain which, at first glance, appears similar to the form we have been discussing. The principal actors once again consist of an individual and collectivity at odds over a wrong that raises a call for an apology as the primary means for moral reparation and social harmony. As before, the Many enjoy the advantages of plurality, while the One stands alone in opposition. Finally, third parties may or may not be drawn into the dispute. Thus it may seem that the two forms are precise mirror images of each other, identical in structure except for the superficial point that in one configuration in the Many are the recipients (or seekers) of an apology, in the other the givers of same. But as is so often the case in social life, apparently minor alterations or reversals of pattern are capable of producing a radically new set of options and constraints. As I shall try and show in what follows, despite the fact that the elements of the two categories are the same, it is the difference in the direction or trajectory of the call and apology that gives this form a unique identity. And it is from this structural difference that all others follow.

From the individual's point of view, the fundamental experiential distinction between the two modes of discourse is perhaps best revealed by contrasting oneiric metaphors. There is, as a close reading of the Jones and Bear cases suggests, a nightmarish or surrealistic quality surrounding a summons and confrontation with a collectivity. Sorrow, a strong but susceptible emotion, tends to become commingled and distracted; apology assumes a formal, programmed character so alien in spirit to its interpersonal counterpart. At the same time, no matter how flimsy or substantial the grounds for the call, no matter how cathartic or therapeutic the experience, there remains an underlying tension that suffuses the accused's world with dark, often violent, hues and images.[24] Under public questioning and security, what was previously taken as self-evident about one's place in the natural order of things becomes problematic and tenuous. An unsettling enough situation in the case of minor transgressions, when core memberships and relationships hang in the balance, disquietude mounts. Obviously, the degree of individual apprehension will vary according to the severity of the offense, moral sensibilities of the offender, power of the collectivity to impose sanctions, and other contingencies. All this notwithstanding, however, I would argue that it is only at the extreme ends of the human moral spectrum—among doves and serpents—that such emotions fail to surface when the One engages an offended and accusatory Many in apologetic discourse.[25]

By sharp contrast, an apology from the Many to the One as a sign of genuine remorse may be likened to a sweet dream come true. For example, is there anyone among us who has not suffered some scarring indignity or unforgettable harm at the hands of an unresponsive, callous, or hubristic collectivity? Consider the hosts of resentful, resigned, and hopeless actors in minor and major social productions doomed to repeat their roles endlessly for want of an apology and the admission of wrongful conduct. And think also of the myriad personal fantasies harbored in which satisfaction, vindication, justice, or grace are finally attained and the world is set right, all because of an apology. In short, when voluntarily given, collective acknowledgment of an injustice to an individual in the form of an apology is a singular and humane achievement. It is rendered all the more so, since, historically, its negative manifestations—coercion, evasion, insensitivity, or just plain indifference—have been the hallmarks of corporate dealings with aggrieved individuals. It is as if the latter were an affront to smooth organizational functioning, inconvenient and irritating human reminders of communal fallibility who, despite their tribulations, must be silenced or ignored. Collectivities, and this is probably a gross understatement, are much more likely to demand expressions of contrition from errant members (or non-members) than to offer them apologies when they are at fault.

Although this form of apology seems to be relatively infrequent in Western societies, it is not unknown or without consequence, especially for those on the receiving end but also for the collective bestowers. Even belated recognition of a wrong can restore the good standing of an individual, serve to amend, and clear the conscience of the Many without, of course, erasing the sufferings of the injured party. When this does happen, the miraculous properties of an apology once more become evident, and life can take on a new meaning. The following account documents one such rare instance and highlights the profound effect of an apology on an individual's state of mind and a corporate entity's sense of honor:

Montreal (CP)—The United Church of Canada finally apologized yesterday to Rev. James Endicott, a Chinese-born missionary who was forced to resign his ministry in 1946 after he was condemned by some church leaders for backing the Chinese Communist revolution.

Endicott, 83 now, said in a telephone interview from Toronto, "*I did not expect to live to see this day . . . I am very grateful.*"

The apology came in a resolution adopted at the church's biennial general council meeting being held here.

Endicott is the son of a former United Church moderator and was a missionary in China for 21 years before he broke with the West China mission board and supported the Chinese Revolution.

As a result back in Canada in 1946 he had to resign from the ministry after he was denounced by Rev. Gerald Bell, then secretary of the mission board.

Bell said it was against the interest of God to speak out against the Chinese nationalist government of Generalissimo Chiang Kai-shek.

Endicott's critics said he should either be expelled from the church, or defrocked.

Endicott remained in the church but started campaigning for world peace and a drawing together of the West and Communist countries.

In 1952, a general council assembly ruled that Endicott did not speak for the United Church after he accused the United States of practicing germ warfare in the Korean War.

After Endicott visited China that year, the federal government threatened to charge him with sedition and treason, but never followed through.

Yesterday's resolution acknowledged that the church had caused him "much personal hurt and anxiety" and apologized for it.

It also recognized that "events in the past 30 years have borne out many of his predictions and prophetic actions on the issue of world peace."

"The present generation of peacemakers owe a great debt" to Endicott's leadership and vision, it said. The resolution "affirms the faithful and courageous contribution he made to the cause of peace and global justice."[26]

By and large, in contrast, the examples of this form I have been able to locate do not evince such candidness or self-abnegation on the part of the Many. Typically, individuals who have been ill used by collective agencies must, when so disposed, exert considerable and sustained effort to receive an apology, no less material compensation when this is in order, with little or no hope of success. Moreover, although such cavalier treatment is commonplace in individual dealings with large or impersonal organizations, it is hardly unknown, though socially less visible, in smaller, more intimate associations such as families, work groups, and communities. As to the former, egregious examples are legion and provide us with further insights into the nature of personal vulnerabilities and institutional ethics and practices. One such, in many ways paradigmatic but with potentially baneful consequences, was reported in the press as follows:

A mouse in the blueberry pie, a bolt in a can of kernel corn, a grasshopper's leg in tomatoes—all sorts of exotic foreign material are found in food from time to time.

If the retailer or manufacturer has any public relations sense at all, he will waste no time in smoothing things over by offering an apology and a free case of whatever it was that contained the offending object.

The customer is happy because he/she got something for nothing. And the company is happy because hopefully now the customer won't tell the whole world about the incident.

That's usually what happens. But not always.

Mrs. Ellis Houliston of 836 McMeans Avenue was eating away on a pork chop one night last week when she felt something sharp in her mouth. She promptly removed what food was in her mouth and on examination discovered a straight pin.

Somewhat shaken but unharmed, Mrs. Houliston took the pin down to her local Safeway store on Kildare Avenue in Transcona where she had purchased the chops. Federal health department officials were called in to investigate, but nothing came of it.

"Because there was not meat surrounding the pin, they didn't feel they could take any legal action," she said.

"I went back to Safeway and I was told I should consider myself lucky that nothing serious happened."

"They said they are taking no responsibility."

Mrs. Houliston said she was offered one pork chop to replace the one with the pin. That was it. No apology, no nothing.

Mrs. Houliston maintains it's not a free side of pork she's after.

"I am just trying to get Safeway to acknowledge their responsibility and that it could have caused serious damage," she said.

If they had done that in the first place and said they were sorry, she says she probably wouldn't have bothered pursuing the matter.[27]

Aside from its local newsworthy aspects—aggrieved and helpless consumer confronts uncaring large company—this incident underscores some of the legal implications of apology from the Many to the One in North America. Specifically, collectivities such as private corporations and businesses, public agencies and bureaucracies, and various other corporate actors are usually reluctant to offer even pro forma apologies to those who have suffered because of human error and oversight, technical failure, administrative breakdowns, incompetence, or sheer indifference. The relative insignificance of apology as a key element in the resolution of conflicts and disputes when corporate entities are at fault stems, for the most part, from the close connection between apology and legal liability. As we have seen, an essential component of a sincere and full apology is that a harmful, unaccountable act did, in fact, occur. In this case, Mrs. Houliston correctly inferred that an apology from Safeway would "acknowledge their responsibility and that it could have caused serious damage," as well as raise the possibility, it should be added, of a lawsuit in lieu of some negative but ephemeral publicity. Hence, because an apology necessarily acknowledges admission and fault (whether in a civil or criminal action), it is likely to be interpreted as acceptance of liability and grounds for compensation by authoritative third parties, in this case, legal officers and agents. The point here is that once we leave the interpersonal or unmediated discursive domain ruled by conscience and an earnest desire for reconciliation, the legal economy imposes a logic that allocates the debits of material damages or punishment and the credits of formal satisfaction or forgiveness. Given these cultural and judicial facts of life, to apologize sincerely is a potentially stupid and costly gesture, especially when the offense is a serious one.

But as a number of legal scholars have pointed out, enlightened judicial intercession and guidance could effectively promote a more peaceful atmosphere and reduce litigation between the Many and the One and between persons. For example, in a comparative study of the Japanese and American legal systems, the authors note that in the former the courts encourage and may even require active efforts by the parties to resolve differences through conciliation and compromise. They also point out that apology figures prominently in the proceedings even when it is not explicitly codified in law. By contrast, in considering the ambiguous and cloudy status of apology in American law, they come to the following conclusion:

> The important point here is that while there are some injuries that cannot be repaired just by saying you are sorry, there are others that can *only* be repaired by an apology. Such injuries are the very ones that most trouble American law. They include defamation, insult, degradation, loss of status, and the emotional distress and dislocation that accompany conflict. To the extent that a place may be found for apology in the resolution of such conflicts, American law would be enriched and better able to deal with the heart of what brought the controversy to public attention. It would also be relieved of some of the pressure to convert all damages into dollars— a pressure that produces absurdly large punitive judgments when a trier of fact sympathetically identifies with the claim of degradation and emotional distress but the economic loss is fictive. More to the point, society at large might be better off and better able to advance social peace if the law, instead of discouraging apologies in such situations by treating them as admissions of liability, encouraged people to apologize to those they have wronged and to compensate them for their losses. Lawsuits may never be filed in such situations.[28]

Although the legal ramifications of apologetic discourse between the Many and the One are clearly important and merit further study, an interesting sociological question remains to be addressed in connection with this form. Initially, let us put it as follows: is it possible for a collectivity, a "Many," as we have broadly formulated it, to apologize to a person? As mentioned earlier, in Japan it is customary for senior officials and executives to offer apologies as well as monetary compensation to those who have been injured by their enterprises or to the victims' kin. We have also noted that although such acts are neither commonplace nor institutionalized in North American culture, where the emphasis is on formal legal procedures and litigation, they nevertheless do occur on occasion, as illustrated by the example of Endicott and of others.[29] It would appear, then, that the answer to our question is, with these qualifications, in the affirmative.

Putting aside the issues of frequency and relative institutionalization, one immediately encounters deeper discursive puzzles, namely, how is an apology formulated in this context and what does it signify? What does it, or can it, render when essentially inanimate, and therefore mute, social entities require human agents to speak on their behalf? Finally, can we speak of collective sorrow and regret in any sense other than metaphorically? Clearly, many important and complex problems are nested in these large questions, but for the moment we shall focus on two separate but related matters that serve to shed further light on the distinctive dynamics of this form of apology. The first has to do with the problematic ontological status of the Many, and the second, with the resolution of this structural ambiguity by the One. Let us consider each in turn.

We have already noted that our usage of the term "collectivity" embraces diverse social units ranging from relatively small primary groups to large secondary associations. Now in linguistic and cognitive terms, we generally have little difficulty in speaking of the sorrow and regret of the Many when the Many in question consist of human actors. For example, a statement to the effect that a family, community, ethnic group, or even nation expressed sorrow or regret over something is not likely to strike us as odd or be dismissed as unwarranted personification. How such social entities go about apologizing for transgressions is another matter that remains to be discussed.

By contrast, as we move to the more *corporate* end of the collective spectrum in the strict sense of the word, that is, legally constituted organizations or bodies with rights, privileges, and liabilities distinct from those of their members, metaphoric speech begins to falter, semantic problems multiply, and existential ambiguities intrude. At the same time, whereas certain human attributes and faculties are routinely and freely attributed to corporate entities or actors, as when we say a company, union, or public bureaucracy is healthy, sick, responsible, greedy, and so on, others do not transfer as easily or without jarring our sensibilities.[30] Among these I would include such emotions as love, hate, shame, guilt, and, all the more telling for our purposes, sorrow and regret. Somehow or other, references to corporate sorrow or remorse ring hollow, sound disingenuous and self-serving, strain credibility, and are strikingly discordant ascriptions and terms that seem to push personification beyond its limits and functions. Such matters are further clouded insofar as suprapersonal entities cannot, by definition, act on their own but only through human agents. If corporate actors, essentially fictive creatures, cannot feel sorrow or regret, this would appear to preclude the kind of apologetic speech produced by real or "natural" persons.[31]

These observations notwithstanding, we have seen, in this section and elsewhere, that collectivities can, do, and, at times, must apologize to persons they have harmed, *in a manner of speaking*. But, and this is crucial, what is this manner of speaking, given the absence of legal and ontological equivalence between the parties? In this case, the formulation of an apology is ruled and constrained by the very nature of the Many. Which is to say that whatever its motive, content, tone, or mode of representation, the apology has a strong tendency to be more or less formal, indirect, allusive, and, in light of its source, addressed to a wider audience as much as it is to the offended person. In the latter sense, it speaks to interested third parties, the wider society, its own institutional history, and posterity. To the extent that all this is so, how do we come then to speak and act *as if* the situation were otherwise? I would submit that when we think of a Many apologizing, we have in mind a single actor capable of conveying a single thought or sentiment in a single and unequivocal voice.

This means that what is required by all concerned, but especially the injured party, is a symbolic and conceptual transformation of the Many in order to generate a form of discourse that effectively negates or obscures the corporate, that is, impersonal and abstract, character of the Many. In other words, the collectivity must constitute itself and be perceived as *a singular entity*, a One in its own right with its own voice. And this suggests that it is only by a literal stretch of the imagination involving metaphorical manipulation or socially induced misrecognition—for the most part unconscious operations—that we allow an apology by the Many or equate such an act with interpersonal apology.[32] What is at stake here, consequently, is not the objective or legal status of corporate actors as such but their moral limits, even though—and this is a cardinal point—the effects of their actions may appear indistinguishable from those of interpersonal apology.[33] For example, the fact that the Reverend Endicott received a belated apology from a corporate entity called "The United Church of Canada" rather than from those directly responsible for his mistreatment did not, as far as we can tell, diminish or dilute his relief and joy.[34] At the same time, what it required of him (and other recipients of collective regrets) was not only patience but a truly remarkable act of anthropomorphizing whereby, for all practical and moral purposes, the Many became a virtual natural person or One.

Apology from the Many to the Many

We come, finally, to the last of the four relations in our typology, apology from the Many to the Many. This form is of particular interest because it is the only one in which individuals do not figure as *principals*. Instead, their primary role is that of official attendants, executants, agents, or emissaries. Since collectivities cannot act (except in a metaphorical sense) and have no voices of their own, they can communicate with each other only via authoritative deputies in conversation that may be described as mutually ventriloquial speech. As our discussion of apology from the Many to the One revealed, although this necessity does not preclude the effective articulation of collective regrets, delegation—double delegation in the present case—challenges a discourse whose semantic code is so deeply rooted in unmediated human relationships. This structural feature, then, will serve as our analytical point of departure for readdressing a number of questions we have touched upon but that remain to be considered more closely. Specifically, how is this discourse shaped and colored by its representative character? How does it differ from interpersonal apology? What can apologetic speech between the Many tell us about the moral capabilities and limits of collectivities? And, finally, what is the nature of its achievement? I shall begin with some general observations about this type of social actor and then attend to the form's discursive entailments and concrete examples.

At first glance, it could be argued that this category merely recapitulates or is no more than a taxonomical variant of interpersonal apology insofar as the social units in question, whatever their relative size, status, or complexity, are formally equivalent. From this point of view, an apology, let us say, between two nations or other collectivities, is essentially the same as one between two natural persons or human beings. While this formulation may be logically tenable, it is sociologically misleading. As I have tried to show in the previous two sections, the fact that collectivities are givers or receivers of apologies profoundly affects the ways in which the principals view each other, conduct themselves, and speak.

At the risk of going over familiar ground, it should be reiterated that the Many, in the broad sense we are using the term, are not simply persons writ large or aggregates of individuals, but *sui generis*, emergent entities with characteristics that set them apart from individuals functioning as sovereign actors.[35] For present purposes, and again focusing on the corporate and institutional end of the collective spectrum, they are best understood as social inventions or creations. In other words, they are artificial and intangible bodies formally founded and sustained by human purposes, efforts, and discourse but with an independent existence, history, and identity as defined by custom or law. Such entities may survive beyond the lives of their members, enjoy special rights and privileges, command vast resources, and wield great power in comparison with individual human actors. In these and other respects, they are as real as anything can be. True enough. But despite all of this, they cannot speak or act on their own. As a consequence, while leaving intact the sequential structure of the apologetic code (breach, call, response, forgiveness), their presence introduces twists and turns, recesses, and peripheries that are either absent or incipient in similar relations between human beings. Although we have alluded to some of these at various points, it is time now for a more systematic examination of the interlocking social, linguistic, and expressive dynamics that give this form its particular timbre.

In the first place, this configuration takes us most fully into a formal, official, and public discursive world. I use the term "formal" here in two distinct but connected senses. On the one hand, the interlocutors are not autonomous persons at liberty to act according to their own moral lights but occupants of institutionally designated offices or positions whose functions are defined and circumscribed by collective goals and interests. At the same time, their status as representatives entails a stylized approach to language and way of speaking that allows little room for the kind of spontaneity, flexibility, or improvisation found in ordinary speech. The wording and tenor of the apology, typically the product of anonymous authors, must be carefully crafted with minimal qualification or elaboration in order to avoid ambiguity or further offense and to ensure the good faith of the offending party. Likewise, as public representatives, those who convey the apology must conform to conventional standards of decorum and protocol. Attention and adherence to formalities are thus intimately linked to the group's honor and integrity and are of paramount importance in this discursive domain. All told, the consummate collective apology is a diplomatic accomplishment of no mean order.

Representation also means that the symbolic efficacy of an apology made by agents ultimately resides in the group that "authorizes and invests it with authority," that is, makes it official and binding.[36] In this respect, the formal hallmark of corporate apologetic speech is what may loosely be termed its "on behalf of" character, something, as we have seen, that is totally out of place between private persons.

Acting as a proxy involves a dual orientation or perspective—one as an authoritative member of the collectivity, the other as an unencumbered individual, assuming, of course, that personal and institutional identities are not completely merged, to the detriment of the former. This differentiation of roles is further reinforced and objectified in a fundamental discursive division evident in virtually all situations in which the Many participate, but especially so in the case of apology. Its salience here derives from the fact that deputative speech is, by definition, derivative and organizationally sanctioned. As such, it takes for granted the distinction it engenders and maintains between "on record" (official, binding, collective) and "off the record" (unofficial, non-binding, personal) statements, positions, sentiments, and commitments.[37] These categories are crucial in this context since an apology proffered without proper credentials, that is, lacking the moral imprimatur of the group, amounts to no apology at all. It means nothing because it represents the unaccredited One and not the mandate of the Many.

Although the formal and official aspects of apology between the Many are important keys for understanding this complex discursive project, they are not the only ones. For above (and including) all else, we are dealing here with speech that is quintessentially *public*. This is its basic dynamic, the organizing and decisive attribute that situates the discourse, determines its mode of expression, and makes it coherent. But the usage "public," in addition to its commonly assigned connotations, has special significance in this instance that has to be spelled out and elaborated.

At an obvious level, although it is possible for corporate actors to conceal their harmful activities, concealment in the face of an offended Many calling for an apology is always problematic and tenuous—all the more so since collective victims, so to speak, have a stake in seeking wider publicity in order to rally support for their cause and document their grievances.[38]

But these are not really the central issues, even though they may play a prominent role in the preliminary events leading up to the offender's response. That is to say, the violation may be committed in relative secrecy, but the apology cannot be so rendered without reducing it to a private exchange that binds neither collectivity. A situation that immediately comes to mind is one in which the violation is public, but the apology between representatives is, for any number of reasons, private. For example, the head of one state apologizes to another *in camera* to reduce political tensions arising from some incident while remaining publicly silent or denying fault. This would not constitute an apology from the Many to the Many in our scheme of things because it is not part of any public record but rather an informal understanding between two individuals. More to the point, once the call for an apology is heeded, its force and meaning reside in the very fact that it is recorded in *a* public domain, whether "public" in these circumstances refers only to the offended collectivity or includes other interested parties.

At the same time, the questions of who is privy to the apology or what is generally known or shared, important in their own right, do not delimit the concept "public" in this discursive context. This is so because they are rooted in, and ruled by, a more elusive dimension of publicity that at once defines and distinguishes this form of apology, namely, to amplify what was said earlier, the primacy of the *record* in regard to the production and registration of the speech. And it is ultimately this necessity, a speech whose sole raison d'être is the record, that takes us to the heart of collective apology. In contrast to unmediated interpersonal relations, where ephemeral words have the power to seal an apology and thus put an end to something that alienates, unrecorded representative speech has no meaning or authority. Consequently, the apology is fashioned for the record and exists only by virtue of its appearance on record. To put it another way, the record, as idea and actuality, determines the preparation and formulation of the apology. This is where we can understand the speech itself; that it appears on public record *is* the apologetic fact.[39]

Thus far, our attention has been centered on the broad structural biases inherent in collective apologetic discourse. But what of the speech itself? Here, too, we find a distinct mode of articulation that differs conspicuously from its interpersonal counterpart. As befits its formal, official, and public character, institutionally licensed and scripted apology tends to be couched in abstract, remote, measured, and emotionally neutral terms.[40] However sincere or faithful to a conciliatory spirit, representative speech composed for the record establishes and preserves a social and hence linguistic distance between those empowered to speak, on the one hand, and the actual protagonists, on the other. These tendencies, it should be noted, are not merely by-products of mediated speech but also stem from the discursive and practical obstacles in addressing a collective bill of particulars that documents numerous personal injuries, deprivations, and suffering, often far removed in time from the present. In light of such difficulties and the need to produce a manageable and effective discourse of record, when regrets by the Many are forthcoming, they are typically expressed in a compressed and summary manner.[41]

Implicit in all of this is yet another aspect of corporate apologetic discourse, or, more aptly, its substantive grounds, that merits at least brief mention. I refer to the emphasis on more or less elaborate systems of record-keeping for assessing the moral claims of other collectivities, something that is normally not encountered in the realm of interpersonal relations except in attenuated form. What I have in mind here, for example, are written, printed, photographic, drawn, or electronically produced materials introduced as evidence of innocence, extenuation, or culpability in response to a call for an apology. It should be recognized that this reliance on records by the Many is not simply a technical matter involving the collecting, storing, and retrieving of information pertaining to the alleged transgression but has more subtle and diffuse effects. Two of these are of immediate interest and dovetail with the other characteristics of this discourse. First, it accords a privileged status to official documents, as opposed to the spoken words and deeds of human actors, and thereby further entrenches a distant and disembodied mode of speech. Second, if the official record defines social reality and is a public representation of the collectivity's moral self-image, what does not appear on record is questionable, dubious, or disqualified.[42]

Throughout the foregoing discussion, interpersonal apology has served as our conceptual point of reference and comparison. And yet its central component, that which is expressed by the apology—*sorrow*—has not been mentioned in connection with collective apology.

It would seem, therefore, that sorrow is ruled out or, at best, perfunctory in light of the formal, official, and public discursive requirements of apology from the Many to the Many. If this is indeed so, does it mean that in comparison with interpersonal apology, the achievement of a collective one is somehow "inferior," so compromised by the necessity of delegation as to be inconsequential in effecting reconciliation? Or that intergroup apology bears so faint a resemblance to the other forms as to call into question its conceptual kinship to them? These are not trivial issues because they challenge the general idea of apology I have put forth and its specific empirical applicability. Moreover, they arise from a more fundamental question encountered elsewhere in our inquiry but not with the clarity manifested in this category: is authentic apologetic discourse restricted to only one mode of speech whose moving force and vital center is sorrow? In order to begin to sort out these theoretical considerations, it will be helpful to look at some concrete examples of collective apology. To this end, and keeping in mind the questions we have broached at each step of the way, let us examine the actual workings, goals, and consequences of this form on its own terms. I shall do this briefly, presenting some fairly straightforward illustrations drawn mainly, but not exclusively, from the sphere of international relations as reported in the press. All are situations in which the resolution of a specific dispute or settling of past scores between collectivities depended, in part or wholly, upon an apology.[43]

In January 1968, the U.S.S. *Pueblo*, an American intelligence vessel, was seized by the North Koreans on the ground that it had violated their territorial waters. The United States denied the charge, claiming the ship was operating in international waters. After ten months of negotiations, the crew (but not the ship) was released when the United States, in a signed statement prepared by the North Koreans, apologized by admitting the violation and giving firm assurances that it would not happen again. Before and after the apology was put on record, American officials vehemently denied the charges, saying the statement was signed under duress and only as a means of freeing the crew. The insistence by the North Koreans on the apology *they had authored* and the anger and frustration over what the Americans viewed as a humiliation underscored the symbolic significance of the apology for both parties. Despite these repudiations, the apology remained on record as an admission of guilt, put an end to the matter, and freed the crew. Moreover, and although this is no more than speculation, it probably led to more caution in the deployment of American vessels in the vicinity of North Korea.

The second example also involves a superpower and smaller nation and in circumstances similar to the first. On 27 October 1981, a Soviet submarine ran aground within Swedish territorial waters near a restricted naval base. Swedish authorities demanded an apology and explanation while rejecting initial Soviet claims that the incursion was unintentional and the result of bad weather and a faulty compass. On 30 October, the Soviet ambassador conveyed unreserved formal regrets to the Swedish foreign minister for the submarine's trespass. This response pleased and surprised Swedish officials since the usual Soviet procedure was to blame individuals and not to apologize formally and without reservation to other governments. After further investigation and interrogation of the vessel's commander, the submarine and crew were released on 6 November. Despite their obvious military superiority, and like the Americans in the *Pueblo* affair, the Soviets were clearly at a disadvantage in their dealings with Sweden. But to attribute their action to sheer expediency would ignore the fact that it was not typical and that it had other consequences. The apology did serve as public acknowledgment of the transgression, smoothed the way for a peaceful solution to an awkward political and military situation, and established a normative precedent—however problematic or binding—for future relations between the two nations.

In August 1983, the United States formally apologized to France for having helped Nazi war criminal Klaus Barbie flee to Bolivia and escape prosecution after World War II. France had been pressing the United States for years to admit its role in Barbie's escape and had finally managed to place him on trial for crimes against humanity after he was brought back to France in February 1983. Barbie, who had lived under an alias for over 30 years, was accused of deporting Jews to death camps and of numerous acts of torture and murder when he headed the Gestapo in Lyons between 1942 and 1944. In the 1950s, France had twice sentenced him in absentia to death. According to a U.S. Department of Justice report, Barbie was protected from war-crime prosecutors after the war when the Army Counter Intelligence Corps recruited him as a spy, lied to the U.S. High Commission in Germany in 1949 as to his whereabouts, and helped him escape to Bolivia. In forwarding the report to France, the State Department expressed deep regrets over the actions that had allowed Barbie to evade French justice for 33 years. A Justice Department official in charge of the report who had recommended that the U.S. apologize said: "This is a matter of decency and of honorable conduct." French authorities welcomed the apology. Needless to say, the political, legal, and diplomatic ramifications of the Barbie affair were much more complicated than this abbreviated account indicates. But of immediate concern are the events leading up to the belated apology and its upshot. Wrongful acts were committed by individuals within the scope of their official capacities. After an extensive investigation and repeated calls for an apology, the U.S. government finally admitted that it was morally responsible for the actions of its agents and expressed regret. The apology thus placed the transgressions on public record and effected a reconciliation between France and the United States.

Moving to an even broader social and temporal context, we turn to Japanese Prime Minister Yasuhiro Nakasone's commemorative address to the United Nations General Assembly on the occasion of the world organization's 40th anniversary on 23 October 1985, during which he apologized to the UN delegates for Japan's role in World War II. "Since the end of that war, Japan has profoundly regretted the ultra-nationalism and militarism it unleashed, and the untold suffering the war inflicted upon peoples around the world and, indeed, its own people," he said. Nakasone added that "having suffered the scourge of war and the atomic bomb, the Japanese people will never again permit the revival of militarism on their soil." In this instance, we have a nation's highest-ranking government official confessing collective guilt, reminding his own people and others of past wrongs, acknowledging the legitimacy of supranational codes of behavior and ethics, and pledging that Japan's future domestic and foreign affairs would be influenced by what had happened. Whatever else this dramatic symbolic gesture meant or achieved, for example, how the Japanese viewed themselves and their position in the world over time, the fact remains that a long-standing silence had been broken; an affirmation of moral responsibility, in the most public of forums, had been made and entered into the historical record.

Our last illustration, like the previous two, concerns an apology arising from events that occurred during World War II. On 10 August 1988, U.S. President Ronald Reagan signed into law a bill offering the nation's apology and authorizing (subject to congressional approval) financial compensation to Japanese Americans who had been interned during the war years. This was the final version of bills passed in the Senate and House of Representatives after five years of hearings, debate, and lobbying. An earlier draft of the House measure that pointedly summarized the general tenor of the bill included the following statement: "The Congress recognizes that a grave injustice was done to both citizens and resident aliens of Japanese ancestry by the evacuation, relocation, and internment of civilians during World War II. On behalf of the Nation, the Congress apologizes." In addition to receiving individual apologies, each eligible internee (estimated to number 60,000 of the 120,000 detained in camps) would receive a tax-free payment of $20,000. The bill further acknowledged that the nation had committed a "grave injustice" and that the relocation and internment program was undertaken "without adequate security reason and without any acts of espionage or sabotage" being recorded. In commenting upon the legislation, Reagan said, "No payment can make up for those lost years. What is most important in this bill has less to do with property than with honor. For here we admit wrong." Leaders of organizations active in implementing the legislation reported that Japanese Americans had reacted with a "collective sigh of relief." Echoing Reagan's sentiments, Ben Takashita of the Japanese American Citizens League said that while the money "could not begin to compensate a person for his or her lost freedom, property, livelihood or the stigma of disloyalty," it showed that the government's apology was "sincere." (Checks and letters of apology from President George Bush were mailed to internees beginning in October 1990.)

This abbreviated inventory—many other examples could be cited —illuminates a number of things about collective apology alluded to earlier. On the practical side, the burden of the apology rests primarily on its corroborative functions: in publicly acknowledging the fact of violation, accepting or fixing responsibility, and implicitly or explicitly promising that similar acts will not be repeated in future. It is only after these matters are placed on record that the formal resolution of the dispute becomes possible.[44] On quite another discursive plane, the very implication of an apology in the collective dialogue, its salience and centrality in the negotiations and proceedings, reveals that issues not subject to a purely utilitarian or material calculation are at stake. These include, for example, corporate honor, prestige, repute, righteousness, and moral censure of the offending party. This much is clear.

But what is not immediately evident in these examples and in others—to return to the question that occasioned this digression— is anything that could unequivocally be construed as sorrow or remorse. At one extreme, what could be further from these concepts than the text the Americans signed in the *Pueblo* affair, which was authored by the North Koreans themselves? Although certainly less egregious than this example, the official declarations of regret in the other cases are, without exception, phrased in measured, distant, and relatively pallid terms. At the same time, there is a parallel dampening and muting of sorrow's reciprocal in the apologetic equation insofar as forgiveness on the part of the aggrieved parties is barely audible, if rendered at all.

Nevertheless, to conclude from these remarks that collective apology amounts to little more than corporate cant, or that the negligible role of sorrow renders it an apology in name only, would betray a serious misunderstanding of what these illustrations exemplify and the unique energy of this form. Why is this so? As we have seen, apologetic speech from the Many to the Many differs markedly from such discourse between persons. But it is the underlying difference, from which all others derive, that we must attend to in assessing its meaning, power, and consequentiality. And precisely because its dynamic is different, this form cannot be evaluated strictly according to its ability to reflect sorrow; for reasons already noted, this is simply not its métier or forte.

Instead, the practical and symbolic import of collective apology has to be judged in terms of the remedial and reparative work it accomplishes. To put it another way, interpersonal apology realizes its potential through sorrow and remorse. Without these, the speech dissolves into a tangle of disclaimers and self-justifications, resulting in a neutralizing detachment from the transgression and the offended party. Thus corroboration is a necessary but insufficient condition for an authentic apology between persons. In stark contrast, *although still within the conceptual purview of what is recognized as interpersonal apology*, the major structural requirement and ultimate task of collective apologetic speech is to put things on record, to document as a prelude to reconciliation. And what goes on record, as our illustrations demonstrate, does not necessarily express sorrow and, except in a pro forma fashion, need not in order to effect reconciliation between collectivities. It is the latter function, then, that is the singular and significant achievement of collective apology.

While these generalizations and observations may help to provide us with a keener appreciation of this complex form, they do not fully account for the rhetorical tensions and ambiguities it is capable of generating and resolving. Nor do the illustrative materials give us much more than a fleeting glimpse of the discursive capacities and constraints of collective apology. What is needed now to flesh out the bare bones of our formulations is a more concrete account that allows us to follow the process from beginning to end. To this purpose, I shall present a detailed description and analysis of an unusually well-documented case of corporate apology involving, once again, the United Church of Canada.

Our story begins with an article published in the *Winnipeg Free Press* of 17 August 1986 under the headline, "United Church apologizes to natives for old wrongs."

SUDBURY, Ont. (CP)—In an emotional ceremony around a traditional bonfire Friday night, the United Church of Canada officially apologized to

Canadian native people for past wrongs inflicted upon them by the church.

"We ask you to forgive us," the church's moderator, Rev. Robert Smith of Vancouver told a gathering of native elders representing Indian tribes across Canada.

"In our zeal to tell you about Jesus Christ, we were blind to your spirituality. We imposed our civilization on you as a condition for accepting our gospel."

"As a result, we are both poorer. We are not what God meant us to be."

"These are not just words. It is one of the most important actions ever taken by the church," Smith said to the Indians, in front of about 300 church members who gathered in a parking lot of Laurentian University for the ceremony.

During the debate on the apology, some delegates expressed concerns the statement unfairly blamed missionaries who tried to convert the natives.

But in the end, only about 12 of 300 delegates voted against the apology. Delegates from Canada's largest Protestant denomination are in Sudbury for a week-long general council, during which the church policy for the next two years will be decided.

Emerging from one of two teepees in the parking lot, Stan McKay, chairman of the church's National Native Council, told the gathering "the happiness felt in the council teepee was almost unbelievable" when it was learned the church would issue an apology.

But Art Solomon, one of the elders, wondered what the United Church members intended to do with it.

Before proceeding, let us pause for a moment to review the historical circumstances leading up to the apology recounted in our text and a follow-up story that appeared about a year later.[45]

The United Church was formed in 1925 by the union of Methodist, Congregational, and Presbyterian bodies. According to *The Canadian Encyclopedia*, it had a confirmed membership of about 870,000 in 1986, a substantial decline since the mid-1960s. The organization is renowned for its strong and often controversial stands on a variety of social and moral issues.

The ostensible impetus for the apology was a reassessment of the role of early Methodist missionaries in proselytizing native peoples and subsequent poor treatment of the latter. According to church officials and delegates, the well-intentioned efforts of the missionaries failed to respect and understand indigenous social and cultural patterns. For the most part, they reflected the intolerant, racist, and paternalistic attitudes of the times. As a consequence, traditional be-liefs, practices, and languages were suppressed and denigrated by church and political authorities.

Over time, native congregations (about 60) were established and constituted separate groups within the larger collectivity which, until 1971, remained the source of clerical leadership for native members. Church membership among indigenous peoples has been declining rapidly in recent decades and has been a matter of great concern to the United Church.

After deliberating these developments, church leaders and dele-gates decided it was time to apologize to native members, as in-dicated in the Reverend Smith's statements. Initially, native leaders responded positively, albeit individually, to the church's overtures and plea for forgiveness. Since the 1986 meeting, native groups have been working toward establishing their own governing body within the United Church and becoming more self-sufficient by ordaining their own ministers and increasing the number of lay leaders.

But our account does not end here. In August 1988, the 32nd Gen-eral Council of the United Church convened at Victoria, British Columbia, two years after Smith's dramatic apology. During a cele-bration of the creation of a separate governing council for native peoples, elder Edith Memnook officially responded to the apology on behalf of native members. As reported in the press:

The representatives of the new All-Native Circle Conference which numbers about 40 congregations and 5,000 members, choosing their words carefully, decided to acknowledge the apology but not to accept it.

"Many of our people have difficulty accepting an apology," said Rev. Alf Dumont . . . who is the newly appointed speaker, or leader, of the conference.

"The church has been instrumental in oppression."

He cited the treatment of native peoples in church boarding schools, where they were forbidden to speak their own language or practice their culture. "These are difficult things to heal."

Nonetheless, several native elders who will be responsible for the direc-tion of the new conference said they were pleased with their new status. "I was too happy, I was crying with emotion," Ms Memnook said minutes after her acknowledgment of the apology was greeted with a standing ovation by the gathering of 400 members.[46]

There was no indication of how the United Church leadership reacted to the belated acknowledgment of the apology.

Although an intricate web of social relationships, replicated in other times and places and familiar to students of colonialism, is revealed in this example, it is the rhetoric of collective apology that concerns us. Specifically, how was this speech shaped, expressed, and received? In this instance, the discourse was the culmination of a complicated set of historical circumstances that at once served to bind and alienate the two groups. First of all, despite their obvious and sharp social disparities and the organizational segregation of the natives, this was essentially an internal matter involving members of the same collectivity. Second, the apology was not the upshot of a single, isolated transgression, but stemmed from long-standing, cumulative offenses that were retrospectively defined as such by both parties. Finally, and here we are entering deep waters, the collective nomination of the posthumous protagonists, that is, the missionaries and their spiritual charges, recast them as primarily symbolic figures whose reconstituted past relations became the occasion for a contemporary confrontation about the future interaction of their representatives and descendants.

Thus far, apart from its particularities, there is nothing especially remarkable about this case. In its bold outlines, it resembles the previous examples of apology from the Many to the Many. And yet, if we attend closely to the language employed and phases of the exchanges, we can begin to see something different unfolding before us. Not, to repeat, a difference in form but one related to the testing of discursive limits and, hence, the unstated grounds of collective speech in this context.

The first indication that we are not wholly within the conventional confines of this form is that the call for an apology did not emanate from the offended Many. Instead, it came from the confessed offenders after much reflection, discussion, and collective soul-searching. Although this could be interpreted as an institutionally self-serving move, it is not a convincing explanation on a number of grounds. This was not, after all, a matter of a small sect fighting for its organizational life and dependent upon native members for survival. Furthermore, the emotional and receptive responses of native leaders to the conciliatory gestures cast further doubt on the skeptical view that purely manipulative or political considerations dictated the apology. But what is perhaps most telling in this regard is that efforts to improve relations with native congregations, whatever their motives, could have been made privately and without resort to a dramatic public apology that, according to our sources, caused some internal dissension. All told, the available evidence—admittedly at a journalistic remove—shows that the overwhelming majority of United Church leaders and delegates came to believe that past wrongs against their native co-religionists had poisoned their relationships and that a contrite, public apology was essential to heal the wounds.

Aside from its disarming effect, the symbolic and practical significance of this kind of initiatory act in remedial negotiations between the Many, especially when one group is more powerful than the other, rests in its ability to alter the terms of discourse. More to the point, a collective *mea culpa*, publicly uttered in response to its own call, simultaneously bespeaks recognition and commitment to a normative domain beyond that of immediate self-interest and effectively shifts the moral burden onto the offended party by focusing upon the issue of forgiveness.[47]

Needless to say, the strategic act of speaking first, of unilaterally and publicly breaking official silence in a dramatic confrontation, would carry little weight if the apology lacked the capacity to move and reconcile. Nor would it register as anything more than an empty gesture in isolation from other elements in the situation. Having thus taken the initiative and, additionally, removed themselves from the official precincts of the conference to deliver their urgent message—the symbolic significance of the site and the makeshift tepee where the meeting took place require no more than noting—the church leaders set the stage for a second movement into the speech itself. Everything came together, as our texts inform us, to create an emotional and intimate atmosphere. At the same time, the occasion demanded that formal, official, and authoritative words be spoken and placed on record; nothing short of this would suffice, given the issue at stake and the representative status of the participants. It is at this juncture in the proceedings that the rhetorical tension generated by the attempt to satisfy the requirements of two discrete forms of discourse, the collective and the personal, becomes evident and, by extension, underscores the question of limits. But we are moving ahead of ourselves. Before considering such meta-discursive issues, let us return to the content and consequences of the apology so as not to lose sight of its practical effects.

To repeat, selectively, in order to highlight and make legible:

> In our zeal to tell you about Jesus Christ, we were blind to your spirituality. We imposed our civilization on you as a condition for accepting our gospel. As a result, we are both poorer. We are not what God meant us to be. These are not just words. It is one of the most important actions ever taken by the church. We ask you to forgive us.

A first reading of these simple, direct, and succinct words unveils the essential features of collective apology. In addressing native members—note the exclusive use of plural forms throughout—the Reverend Smith, speaking on behalf of the United Church, admits the primal transgression in general terms, accepts corporate responsibility, implies sorrow, and asks for forgiveness to clear the air and establish harmonious relations. Thus the language has total institutional authority.

By contrast, although the initial response to the overture was positive, it was personal, individual, and without official sanction. For example, the Reverend McKay, a native minister and leader, said: "The happiness felt in the council tepee was almost unbelievable." A year later, McKay commented in more detail:

> For all of us the apology was very moving. For many older people who remember as children the suppression of the old ways there was deep sense of liberation.
>
> The fact that they did not understand us and that mistakes were made does not cause us to diminish their [missionaries] contribution and their good will. We hold them in very high regard. The era of mission to native people is over.

As we have seen, it was not until two years after the church's apology and plea for forgiveness that an official reply was received.

And although many organizational changes had occurred during the interim, native leaders, "choosing their words carefully, decided to acknowledge the apology, but not to accept it." A nice touch and display of moral tact that served to credit the apology with good will without disregarding the gravity of past and recent indignities by forgiving too easily or quickly and thus releasing the church from the consequences of what it had done and condoned. In this case, the immutability of collective memory prevented the washing clean of what had happened, the emotively charged and conciliatory tone of the public exchanges notwithstanding.

Whatever the residues of private doubt, anger, or indifference following the apology and its "acknowledgment," there can be little question as to its decisive role in venting the source of mutual disquietude and paving the way for structural changes in the relations between the two groups. And although the collective apology did not accomplish all it set out to do, it was instrumental in bringing about social harmony.

So much for the power of the United Church's apology to stimulate a rapprochement between the two parties. What about its meta-discursive aspects, that is, the extent to which it reveals the inherent difficulty in transcending the limits of collective apologetic discourse? It is in this context, where the form and content of the speech intersect and overlap, that the logic of this form is brought into sharp relief by our example. The crux of the matter involves the church's attempt to satisfy the requirements of two related, but incompatible, types of discourse within the confines of the same speech without neutralizing their respective authority. On the one hand, the collective apology to the native peoples speaks, *as it must*, in an official, solemn voice for the record. And so it does. At the same time, the speech tries to inject a colloquial and urgent sense of spontaneity, an off-the-record quality, in what it bespeaks. In so doing, a subtle but definite tension is created. The clue to this tension, the self-conscious recognition of having reached the limits of the collective testimonial and yet falling short of the desired effect, is revealed in the spare and pointed rhetorical flourish, *"These are not just words."* Such an emphatic, reiterative, and potentially subversive utterance, commonplace in ongoing interpersonal relations but exceptional in one-time, formal discourse between corporate actors, is telling because it signals a break in elocutionary mood and alerts us to the existence of multiple levels of meaning. Perhaps most important, it focuses the issue of the discursive bounds of representative speech and, by extension, the moral capacities of collectivities. By way of concluding our discussion of apology from the Many to the Many, therefore, let us briefly consider the implications of this terse and seemingly unremarkable rhetorical formula.

In purely structural or linguistic terms, this self-reflexive device constitutes part of the main speech while deliberately partitioning or distancing itself from it. In effect, the disclaimer endeavors to amplify the motives and content of the apology from a seemingly objective or external perspective, and invites those whom it addresses to do the same. But this break in the discursive frame—akin in some ways to the literary technique of authorial intrusion—does much more than comment on its own speech. It also introduces a personal tone, an unofficial, emphatic, and human voice, as it were, into the official, impersonal public record. On another, yet cognate, semantic level, the negatory insistence that *"these are not just words"* seeks to confirm the earnestness of the institutional pleas for understanding and forgiveness. What follows this succinct and pregnant utterance, *"It is one of the most important actions ever taken by the church,"* further complicates matters by explicitly distinguishing between *what* was said and the fact that it *was* said.

Potential ambiguities and mishearings abound. But this is not the place to pursue them or to engage in an extended hermeneutical treatment of our texts. For present purposes we need only note that this rhetorical stance posits an alternative interpretation of what it says, since it would be meaningless in the absence of opposition or contrast. In this instance, the assertions (*"These are not . . . by the church"*) simultaneously underscore and strive to rerender the formal, abstract, and general tone of the official representations, thereby admitting the possibility or truth of what they so vigorously deny: that these are just words.[48] And it is precisely in such a strained interplay of dual orientations, of different voices, of competing and complementary modes of speaking, that this meta-communicative disclamation illuminates not only the case at hand but the organizing dynamic of collective apology. It inadvertently registers, with ingenuous clarity, that the principal function of the apology—all collective apology, for that matter—has little, if anything, to do with sorrow or sincerity but rather with putting things on a public record. This, as I have argued, is collective apology's distinctive capacity, its ordinary limits, and the ultimate source of its power to remedy and conciliate, if not completely to heal. Thus to demand more of the form is to mistake its task and logic. So it is that the Reverend Smith's impassioned addendum, among its other significations, articulates the frustration of having come up against the limits of its own speech. It is only with the cool, careful, and reflective response to the apology by the offended that we come full circle to the objective conditions and consequences of this discourse. After the heady emotional displays, celebrations, and exuberance surrounding the exchange, the indelible remains on the collective record are the apology and its acknowledgment.

5. Conclusions

In this extended prolegomenon, we have ranged over a considerable expanse of human experience in our attempt to chart an elusive but vital social presence. Elusive, owing to the ephemerality of its essential medium, and vital because of its capacity to move and restore. Since the detailed formulations and illustrative materials upon which this account of apology rests have been presented in the previous chapters, further qualification or elaboration would serve little purpose at this point. Consequently, I shall confine these concluding remarks to a brief recapitulation of the core argument, identifying some problems for further investigation and considering the broader implications of this study.

Apology: Structural and Affective Dimensions

Apology, taken as a speech act, a sign, in dyadic interaction between the primordial social categories of Offender and Offended, has been approached from two distinct but complementary perspectives. The first focuses upon the structural context in which apologetic discourse is embedded and thus intersects and addresses the basic sociological questions of membership, conformity, and social order.

In this domain, role relationships and their accompanying rights and obligations, rules, and institutional imperatives are paramount in shaping the perceptions and expectations of the participants. As we have seen, the production of a socially valid apology entails the knowing and willful violation of a mutually binding norm that defines those affected as members of a moral community. The latter, for our purposes, may or may not coincide with group membership in a strict sociological sense.[1] The offense, that is, may be judged as a violation of popular standards of propriety or morality, as when it is said that "decent, considerate persons do not act in such ways," or as a departure from a designated group's values and norms as, for example, "a devout Christian, members of our family, etc., do not do, say, or think such things." In either case, it follows that the intensity of disapproval, the severity of sanctions, and the extent to which the offender's membership or general moral standing is called into question will depend upon prevailing distinctions between minor and serious normative breaches. Of interest here, then, are socially patterned and objectified definitions of what constitutes an apologizable offense and how one is expected to speak to it.

Correlatively, our second analytical emphasis shifts attention from the social scaffolding of apology, as it were, to its experiential dynamics and structure. The foci in this connection are the initial stirrings of conscience and inner discourse that arise once the experience of misconduct registers subjectively in response to the sharp and animating sting of *sorrow*. It is this, itself a social product, that links, mobilizes, and rules our receptivity to the call for an apology as a necessary prelude to relief and resolution. As we have seen, the provenance and strength of the call, whether it emanates primarily from within or without, whether soft or loud, are matters that will vary from one situation to another. What remains an essential constant at this stage of the process, however, is the wrongdoer's responsiveness in terms of sorrow, the motor and organizing principle of apology.

But interior probing, interrogation, and anguish are not enough to restore an offender to a state of social grace or put things right. This is so, as we have repeatedly stressed, because they tend to resolve themselves into a circular monologue that quickly reaches its psychodynamic and discursive limits and then is forced back upon itself in tedious and fruitless repetition. Until these inchoate feelings and ruminations surface, purged of all traces of self-pity and, most important, articulated in the presence of the offended other, they serve only as soliloquies with little or no consequence or meaning. As one astute observer pointedly reminds us in this context:

Feelings, emotions, thoughts and ideas become clear and are grasped only after they are expressed in sentences bearing a logical and grammatical structure. As long as one's thoughts remain repressed, as long as one has not brought them out into the open, no matter how sublime or exalted they may be, they are not truly yours; they are foreign and elusive. "The heart is deceitful above all things, and it is exceedingly weak—who can know it?" (Jeremiah 17:9). Jeremiah did not mean that one cannot know what is in the heart of others and others cannot know what is in your heart, but that man does not know for sure what is in his own heart until his feelings and thoughts become crystallized and are given shape and form in the usual modes of expression. Repentance contemplated, and not verbalized, is valueless.[2]

Thus the second-order response to the call requires nothing less than an oral apology. In this recitation, the offender acknowledges full responsibility for the transgression, expresses sorrow and contrition for the harm done, seeks forgiveness from the offended party, and implicitly or explicitly promises not to repeat the offense in future. Finally, the discursive loop is closed by the forgiveness of the offender, which symbolizes reconciliation and allows for the resumption of normal social relations.

Apology and Further Lines of Inquiry

What is elided, as much as what is summarized, in the foregoing synopsis alerts us to a number of issues that call for more detailed empirical examination and theoretical attention as further steps in deepening our understanding of apology. In what follows, I simply mention, rather than analyze, some of these. First, although we have alluded to apology in other cultures, with specific reference to Japan, our focus throughout has been on its forms and meanings in contemporary Western societies. To broaden our comprehension of this important social phenomenon, cross-cultural and historical studies, as well as more work on comparative linguistics, are obviously in order.

Second, we need to know a great deal more than I have indicated about the pedagogy of apology within the wider area of moral or deontic socialization. Our preliminary discussion has assumed the ongoing involvement of a committed and competent adult authority figure. But what if none is available or the general norm of apology is absent or so compromised and diluted as to negate the efforts of potential socializing agents? And what, if any, influence is exerted in cultivating an appreciation of the remedial aspects of apology in different social environments, for example, the family, peer groups, schools, and the mass media? As we have suggested, the teaching and learning of apologetic discourse are complex projects that begin in childhood but do not end there. Consequently, their structural determinants and correlates clearly merit further investigation.

Third, although I have referred frequently to forgiveness as a crucial element in the apologetic equation, this mysterious and unpredictable faculty has not been adequately addressed or formulated. If, as I have argued, sorrow is the energizing force of apology, then what moves the offended party to forgive? In historical and cross-cultural terms, what is deemed forgivable and unforgivable? While Arendt has provided us with a thoughtful analysis of the consequences of forgiveness in resolving moral impasses and dealing with secular transgressions, its social and psychodynamic *sources* have been relatively neglected. In other words, to complement and enrich the account of apology we have been trying to develop, we stand in need of a sociology and phenomenology of forgiveness.

Fourth, our discussion of interpersonal apology has tended to overshadow the other forms involving collectivities—the One to the Many, the Many to the One, and the Many to the Many. But as our examples clearly show, it is precisely in such public confrontations that the negative implications of apology are likely to manifest themselves. Specifically, membership in a moral community may be maintained by deliberately offending some despised group or subordinate person. In such cases, one's claim to membership would be invalidated by anything remotely resembling an apology. At the same time, the willingness and ability to apologize in these circumstances would serve as a sensitive indicator of changing attitudes and perceptions. What all this suggests is that a closer inspection of these other forms would, among other things, seek to specify the conditions under which in-groups and out-groups (or their members) apologize to each other as members of *different* moral communities.[3]

Finally, I bring this abbreviated inventory to an arbitrary close, not with yet another omission or understatement but with reference to a topic that has haunted our discussion at virtually every point: specifically, the conceptual, procedural, and linguistic affinities between secular apology and religious confession. If, as repeatedly stressed, an authentic, sincere apology cannot be understood or formulated as an isolated and independent speech act, the same holds true for genuine full confession, given its canonical and sacramental significance. Both the apology and the confession are critical, central moments within larger moral economies whose narrative phases are sequentially parallel. Just as apology is bracketed by a call and forgiveness following a violation, so is confession by contrition and absolution. Needless to say, attending to such similarities is not to ignore important differences in confession that stake out a distinctive discursive territory within the confines of apology that cannot be mapped as mere "variants." For example, when we confess, we do so as members of a moral and *spiritual* community; we confess *sins* in a quest for purification, reconciliation, and personal salvation; and, at least in Christian versions of the sacrament, we confess to God in the presence of an authoritative and mediating *agent*. These, then, are some of the points of convergence and divergence that remain to be considered in greater detail. But not here.[4]

It would be tempting, and perhaps comforting, to conclude our discussion on a moralistic plane, extolling the panacean qualities of apology and forgiveness in settling social conflicts. It would also be naive and simplistic. As we have seen in a variety of contexts, there are acts in the moral spectrum that are beyond forgiveness, individual and collective actors apparently impervious to sorrow, and countervailing institutional imperatives that can effectively silence such speech. Nor, following another optimistic line, can these complex human faculties be reduced to formulas or catch phrases in the service of another therapeutic promise without neutering them. But in between these extremes, in the ordinary and dramatic spaces of human life, a recognition, literally a reknowing of the grounds and potential of apologetic discourse, must precede its praxis. And it is ultimately in these terms, then, that I ask the thoughtful reader to judge the merits and shortcomings of this effort.

REFERENCE MATTER

NOTES

Chapter 1

1. The seminal sociological formulation of apology is Erving Goffman's terse but influential discussion in *Relations in Public*, pp. 113–14, in the context of "remedial interchanges." I shall indicate, later, how the perspective taken in this work differs from his. The studies of the topic I have been able to locate closely follow or elaborate upon Goffman's approach. See, for example, Schlenker and Darby, "The Use of Apologies," and Darby and Schlenker, "Children's Reactions to Apologies," as well as Nagano, "'How to Say I'm Sorry'"; Wagatsuma and Rosett, "The Implications of Apology"; and Haley, "Comment." In the area of sociolinguistics, see the following in Coulmas, *Conversational Routine*: Coulmas, "'Poison to Your Soul'"; Fraser, "On Apologizing"; and Edmondson, "On Saying You're Sorry." See also Blum-Kulka, House, and Kasper, *Cross-Cultural Pragmatics*.

2. In these connections, a national Gallup poll on forgiveness conducted in 1989 found that three-fourths of American men and women surveyed said that they would apologize if they hurt someone else, but women were far more likely to ask for forgiveness. Moreover, twice as many men (13 percent) as opposed to women (6 percent) said they would try and get even in some way with the person who hurt them. "Women More Likely to Seek Forgiveness; Men Want to Get Even," *Post-Standard* (Syracuse, N.Y.), 4 March 1989. As will be repeatedly documented in this inquiry, apologies are every-

where and without exception normatively situated and regulated. Of course, this presupposes collective recognition of the idea or concept of apology on the part of members of a moral community as one possible and expected response to a violation as opposed to others, e.g., hiding, denying, rationalizing. To apologize is thus to conform to a rule stating that, under certain conditions, an apology is in order. So an apology bespeaks a commitment to two normative orders: to conform to the general norm, we must acknowledge that we have violated another norm. The general norm, in turn, calls for a type of self-punishment and revelation as a form of conformity.

3. There is an apposite distinction in law between offenses involving the community, no matter how indirectly, or regardless of the victim's predilection to forgive and forget, and torts (civil actions), which allow for somewhat greater leeway for the wishes of the injured party. There is also an intermediate category, *damnum absque injuria*, i.e., "Loss, hurt, or harm without injury in the legal sense, that is, without such breach of duty as is redressible by an action. A loss which does not give rise to an action or damages against the person causing it." *Black's Law Dictionary* (St. Paul, Minn.: West Publishing Co., 1979), p. 354.

4. "Without being forgiven, released from the consequences of what we have done, our capacity to act would, as it were, be confined to one single deed from which we could never recover; we would remain the victims of its consequences forever, not unlike the sorcerer's apprentice who lacked the magic formula to break the spell." Arendt, p. 237. In this connection, see also Scheler, "Repentance and Rebirth."

5. Bierce, p. 12.

6. *Winnipeg Free Press*, 21–27 May 1980.

7. *Winnipeg Free Press*, 17–18 November 1980.

8. "Every established order tends to produce (to very different degrees and with very different means) the naturalization of its own arbitrariness." Bourdieu, p. 164.

9. Or what Gerbner calls "hidden curricula," i.e., lesson plans that no one teaches but everyone learns. Gerbner, "Teacher Image and the Hidden Curriculum." Bourdieu's observations on unformulated and unformulatable cultural assumptions and euphemisms that "go without saying because they come without saying" also address this point. Bourdieu, pp. 167–71.

10. On the problematics of binding commitments, see Goode, "Norm Commitment and Conformity."

11. On meta-rules and meta-communication, see Bateson, *Steps to an Ecology of Mind*.

Chapter 2

1. Austin, "A Plea For Excuses," p. 182. Not all of which, of course, find their way into lexicons.

2. *Origins: A Short Etymological Dictionary of Modern English* (New York: Macmillan, 1977), p. 347.

3. 1933 ed. (vol. I, p. 1888).

4. *The Random House Dictionary of the English Language: Second Edition—Unabridged* (New York: Random House, 1987), p. 99.

5. This interpretation of the differing contexts of accounts and apologies owes much to Arendt's perceptive discussion of forgiveness and vengeance, although her assertion that vengeance is a "natural" reaction to transgression is questionable.

> Forgiveness is the exact opposite of vengeance, which acts in the form of re-acting against an original trespassing, whereby far from putting an end to the consequences of the first misdeed, everybody remains bound to the process, permitting the chain reaction contained in every action to take its unhindered course. In contrast to revenge, which is the natural, automatic response to transgression and which because of the irreversibility of the action process can be expected and even calculated, the act of forgiveness can never be predicted; it is the only reaction that acts in an unexpected way and thus retains, though being a reaction, something of the original character of action. Forgiving, in other words, is the only reaction which does not merely re-act but acts anew and unexpectedly, unconditioned by the act which provoked it and therefore freeing from its consequences both the one who forgives and the one who is forgiven. Arendt, pp. 240–41.

6. Cf. Foucault, pp. 61–62:

> The confession is a ritual of discourse in which the speaking subject is also the subject of the statement; it is also a ritual that unfolds within a power relationship, for one does not confess without the presence (or virtual presence) of a partner who is not simply the interlocutor but the authority who requires the confession, prescribes and appreciates it, and intervenes in order to judge, punish, forgive, console, and reconcile; a ritual in which the truth is corroborated by the obstacles and resistances it has had to surmount in order to be formulated; and finally, a ritual in which the expression alone, independently of its external consequences, produces intrinsic modifications in the person who articulates it: it ex-

onerates, redeems, and purifies him; it unburdens him of his wrongs, liberates him, and promises him salvation.

7. For an informative discussion of these points, see McHugh, "A Common-Sense Perception of Deviance." See also Austin, "A Plea for Excuses"; Scott and Lyman, "Accounts"; Hewitt and Stokes, "Disclaimers"; Snyder, Higgens, and Stucky, *Excuses*; and Semin and Manstead, *The Accountability of Behavior*.

8. *The Concise Oxford Dictionary*, 6th ed., p. 943. Cf. the first entry in *The Compact Edition of the Oxford English Dictionary* (Oxford: Oxford University Press, 1971), p. 2473: "To remember, think of, (something lost) with distress or longing."

9. A balance must be struck between the nature of the relationship, the severity of the violation, and the fault of the offender. Such delicate moral transactions are always in danger of degenerating into displays of egocentric histrionics, especially, as we shall see later, in public apologies. "Self-blame constitutes an exquisite and expensive form of self-praise. No matter how severe the adjectives, the conversation remains fixed on the subject of supreme interest and importance." Lapham, p. 298. Although regret may also be present in accounts, it is not, I would argue, central because one's energy is invested in deflecting attention elsewhere so as to minimize culpability. Thus, when we attempt to explain, disclaim, or excuse, it is not uncommon to preface our remarks with an expression of sorrow. A small, but telling, linguistic cue that an account rather than an apology is forthcoming is the use of "but" following the expression of sorrow. Regret in these instances may be genuine but incidental, if not perfunctory.

10. One of the few studies of such matters asked college students to project their reactions to hypothetical situations in which they harmed a stranger in a public place. The researchers systematically varied the responsibility of the offender and the severity of the consequences. When responsibility and severity were defined as minimal, perfunctory concern was expressed. By contrast, under conditions of high responsibility and serious effects, informants were most likely to say that they would elaborate their responses with statements of sorrow and remorse, offers of help and redress, self-castigation, and explicit pleas for forgiveness. In formulating a somewhat different view of apology, I shall try and indicate why self-castigation and restitution as they are conceptualized and operationalized in this study (and elsewhere) are not necessary elements of the apologetic mode. Schlenker and Darby, "Children's Reactions to Apologies."

11. Paul L. Montgomery, "Albert Speer, 76, Architect of Hitler's Nazism Is Dead," *International Herald Tribune*, 13 September 1981.

12. Once again, Arendt's perspicacious remarks on forgiveness and punishment illuminate much with respect to such dark deeds. Since her primary concern is with exculpation and unwitting trespasses, she does not consider the role of apology. Nevertheless, it is clear that "radically evil" actions are not only beyond the faculty of forgiving but also that of apologizing, as the Speer case reminds us.

> The alternative to forgiveness, but by no means its opposite, is punishment, and both have in common that they attempt to put an end to something that without interference could go on endlessly. It is therefore quite significant, a structural element in the realm of human affairs, that men are unable to forgive what they cannot punish and that they are unable to punish what has turned out to be unforgivable. This is the true hallmark of those offenses which, since Kant, we call "radical evil" and about whose nature so little is known, even to us who have been exposed to one of their rare outbursts on the public scene. All we know is that we can neither punish nor forgive such offenses and that they therefore transcend the realm of human affairs and the potentialities of human power, both of which they radically destroy wherever they make their appearance. Here, where the deed itself dispossesses us of all power, we can indeed only repeat with Jesus: "It were better for him that a millstone were hanged about his neck and he cast into the sea." Arendt, p. 241.

13. "But what is this self? It is the sum of everything we remember. Thus, what terrifies us about death is not the loss of the future but the loss of the past. Forgetting is a form of death ever present within life. . . . A nation which loses its awareness of its past gradually loses itself. And so the political situation has brutally illuminated the ordinary metaphysical problem of forgetting, that we face all the time, every day, without paying attention. Politics unmasks the metaphysics of private life, private life unmasks the metaphysics of politics." Kundera, pp. 234–35.

14. As Samuel Johnson observed, "Men more frequently require to be reminded than informed."

15. For a superlative analysis of the emotion of shame, see Schneider, *Shame, Exposure, and Privacy*. His distinction between discretion-shame (before the act) and disgrace-shame (after the act) parallels our point about thinking like a member, i.e., recognizing inviolable limits and acting (apolo-

gizing) after a violation. "Being ashamed [shame as disgrace] is a more ambivalent phenomenon than the sense of shame. If discretion-shame sustains the personal and social ordering of the world, disgrace-shame is a painful experience of the disintegration of one's world. A break occurs in the self's relationship with itself and/or others. An awkward, uncomfortable space opens up in the world. The self is no longer whole, but divided. It feels less than it wants to be, less than its best it knows itself to be. Disgrace-shame is *painful, unexpected*, and *disorienting*" (p. 22, Schneider's italics).

16. Which is not to say that such offers and avowals, no matter how unrealistic given the element of uncertainty in human affairs, are not made or invited, but to question whether they are essential components of apology. There is also the danger that the energy invested in such professions may get in the way of regret, overpower it, and hence miss the point of apology.

17. A "speech act" is defined as "any of the acts that may be performed by a speaker in making an utterance, as stating, asking, requesting, advising, warning, or persuading, considered in terms of the content of the message, the intention of the speaker, and the effect on the listener." *The Random House Dictionary of the English Language*, p. 1833. See also Austin, *How to Do Things with Words*, and Searle, *Speech Acts*.

18. The qualification "oral" is not absolute and does allow for the conveying of an apology through, say, sign language or other forms of non-oral communication. Nor do I wish to ignore written apologies, apologies by telephone, etc. I stress speech in the conventional sense and co-presence because they most forcefully combine to minimize, if not altogether eliminate, ambiguity and alternative perceptions, e.g., mistaking the apology for an account, as well as demonstrating the earnestness of the suppliant. Of course, the apologetic speech itself is part of a larger interactional frame that includes both oral and non-oral cues and markers such as vocal nuances, postures, the presence of witnesses, and even facial expressions that can affect its presentation and reception. Regarding the importance of ocular evidence of remorse, consider the following newspaper story, "Look of Regret Frees Jenkins?", *Winnipeg Free Press*, 19 December 1980:

BRAMPTON, Ont. (CP)—Fergie Jenkins, right-handed pitcher for the Texas Rangers of baseball's American League, was given an absolute discharge yesterday on a charge of possessing cocaine.

The absolute discharge means he will have no criminal record.

Jenkins, four times Canadian athlete of the year and described by his lawyer as a national hero, was charged Aug. 25 when three ounces of cocaine were found in his luggage at nearby Toronto International Airport. Two charges of possessing marijuana and hashish were dropped.

Provincial Court Judge Gerald Young, who deliberated for two hours before passing sentence, said he could not help noticing Jenkins's look of remorse during the trial.

19. Needless to say, the process may be short-circuited, interrupted, postponed, or abruptly broken off. In addition, the wronged party may unilaterally forgive before the offender actually apologizes. Or, as with Judas' betrayal of Jesus, the expression of repentance may never reach the victim (Matthew 27: 3–5). In these instances, some elements of apology are present, but there is clearly another form of discourse taking place.

20. Unlike accounts, apologies between individuals in Western cultures—collectivities are another matter and will be discussed in due course—cannot be delegated or given by proxy without radically altering their meaning, undermining their moral claims, and raising serious questions about the membership status and competence of the offender. Since accounts appeal to reasons that seek to detach us (partially or totally) from the consequences of our acts, our immediate presence, though desirable or unavoidable, is not essential to their task. Although others may urge us to offer, accept, or refuse apologies, i.e., to acknowledge and respond to a call, we stand alone and have to speak for ourselves. As opposed to an account, the core purpose of an apology is reinstatement.

21. *Interfaces of the Word*, p. 21.

22. Ong, *The Presence of the Word*, pp. 124–25.

23. *The Amy Vanderbilt Complete Book of Etiquette*, p. 522.

24. Vanderbilt, p. 477.

25. Grounded upon what McHugh calls "conventionality" and "theoreticity," i.e., that the action was not inevitable and the actor was knowingly willful. "These two criteria of responsibility—'It might have been otherwise' and 'He knows what he's doing'—are conventionality and theoreticity of acts, respectively. Whether our interest is in killing, boredom, psychosis, bureaucratic indifference, lying, alienation, disingenuousness, totalitarianism, stupidity, or delinquency, we first assess the possibility that a particular act needn't have occurred at all, whether it is conventional; and then if the agent knew what he was doing, whether it is theoretical." McHugh, pp. 152–53. These criteria are equally and particularly pertinent to apologies.

26. "Miss Manners," *Washington Post*, 7 February 1982.

27. Martin, p. 474.

28. Martin, p. 475.

29. Post, *The New Emily Post's Etiquette*, p. 98.

30. As is clearly enunciated in Martin's jacket notes: "Her book is correct and complete, and the reader who obeys it will be able to proceed in an orderly fashion from birth to death without making a single false move."

31. For an extensive and informative discussion of such texts and related topics, see Elias, *The Civilizing Process*, and Nicolson, *Good Behaviour*. Elias and Nicolson are indispensable sources for those interested in the history of manners and etiquette. Unfortunately, these otherwise valuable works have little or nothing to say about apology. For an illuminating polemic on the connections between morality and etiquette, see Martin and Stent, pp. 237–54.

32. "Action and speech are so closely related because the primordial and specifically human act must at the same time contain the answer to the question asked of every newcomer: 'Who are you?' This disclosure of who somebody is, is implicit in both his words and his deeds; yet obviously the affinity between speech and revelation is much closer than that between action and revelation, just as affinity between action and beginning is closer than that between speech and beginning, although many, and even most acts, are performed in the manner of speech. Without the accompaniment of speech, at any rate, action would not only lose its revelatory character, but, and by the same token, it would lose its subject, as it were; not acting men but performing robots would achieve what, humanly speaking, would remain incomprehensible. Speechless action would no longer be action because there would no longer be an actor, and the actor, the doer of deeds, is possible only if he is at the same time, the speaker of words. The action he begins is humanly disclosed by the word, and though his deed can be perceived in its brute physical appearance and without verbal accompaniment, it becomes relevant only through the spoken word in which he identifies himself as the actor, announcing what he does, has done, and intends to do." Arendt, pp. 178–79.

33. On liminality and rites of passage, see van Gennep, *The Rites of Passage*, and Turner, *The Ritual Process*, especially chap. 3, "Liminality and Communitas," pp. 94–130.

34. Although, as noted earlier, it may also signal other kinds of changes, such as what constitutes an apologizable offense. Thus apologies are not necessarily conservative. In this important context, see Martin and Stent's observations on changing attitudes and regulations with regard to smoking (pp. 246–47). And more directly to the point are the following comments

on apology and the legal system in Japan: "This repeated emphasis on the conservative impact of the apology neglects its role in the process of social change. The plaintiffs in the pollution and drug-related lawsuits did not seek apologies by the government or the defendant firms as a means of maintaining the status quo or preserving social harmony. They instead demanded apologies as a recognition of redefined social norms and as an act of submission to a shifting hierarchical order. The apologies acknowledged the legitimacy of protest and protesters." Haley, p. 503.

35. "In contrast to economic commodities, the benefits involved in social exchange do not have an exact price in terms of a single quantitative medium of exchange, which is another reason why social obligations are unspecific. It is essential to realize that this is a substantive fact, not simply a methodological problem. It is not just the social scientist who cannot exactly measure how much approval a given helpful action is worth; the actors themselves cannot precisely specify the worth of approval or of help in the absence of a money price. The obligations individuals incur in social exchange, therefore, are defined only in general, somewhat diffuse terms. Furthermore, the specific benefits exchanged are sometimes primarily valued as symbols of the supportiveness and friendliness they express, and it is the exchange of the underlying mutual support that is the main concern of the participants." Blau, pp. 94–95. For a critique and elaboration of social exchange theories (including Blau's), see Goode, *The Celebration of Heroes*, especially the preface and chaps. 1–3. The seminal sociological work on this topic remains Homans, *Social Behavior*.

36. Or succumb to a secular version of what is referred to as the problem of "scrupulosity" in the domain of religious confession. To wit: "The psychological disturbance known as 'scrupulosity' is apparently most common in Roman Catholic populations [and] . . . is manifest in obsessive fears that past sins have not been properly confessed or were not understood by the confessor." Hepworth and Turner, p. 48. In the case of apology, this would amount to a crucial, but self-defeating, shift in linguistic and affective focus from the victim to the offender. While there are some obvious and broad parallels between apology and piacular confession, including a shared terminology, the two are not equivalent. For example, the sacrament of penance (or, more recently, "reconciliation") includes contrition, confession, satisfaction, and absolution. As I have tried to show, satisfaction and especially acts of penance externally imposed are not central to apology. More important, whereas a valid confession requires an authoritative intermediary (at least in the Catholic and Orthodox churches) empowered to give absolution, an

apology demands direct dealings between the parties, and the faculty of forgiveness resides exclusively in the offended one. Auricular confession, a rich
topic with a voluminous literature, is beyond the scope of the present essay.

37. Campbell, p. 309. See also Wyatt-Brown, *Southern Honor*.

38. Georg Simmel's astute observations on the cohesive effects of gratitude are, *mutatis mutandis*, apposite to apology as a form of symbolic exchange. After stressing that gratitude supplements the legal order in social
relations where there is no external necessity for its expression, i.e., where
legal rules cannot enforce or guarantee reciprocity, or where equivalence of
exchange is irrelevant, he goes on to say (in "Faithfulness and Gratitude,"
pp. 388–89):

> Beyond its first origin, all sociation rests on a relationship's effect which
> survives the emergence of the relationship. An action between men may
> be engendered by love or greed of gain, obedience or hatred, sociability
> or lust for domination alone, but this action usually does not exhaust
> the creative mood which, on the contrary, somehow lives on in the
> sociological situation it has produced. Gratitude is definitely such a con-
> tinuance. It is an ideal living-on of a relation which may have ended
> long ago, and with it, the act of giving and receiving. Although it is
> a purely personal affect, or (if one will) a lyrical affect, its thousand-
> fold ramifications throughout society make it one of the most powerful
> means of social cohesion. It is a fertile emotional soil which grows con-
> crete actions among particular individuals. But much more: although
> we are often unaware of its fundamentally important existence, and
> although it is interwoven with innumerable other motivations, never-
> theless, it gives human actions a unique modification or intensity: it
> connects them with what has gone before, it enriches them with the ele-
> ment of personality, it gives them the continuity of interactional life. If
> every grateful action, which lingers on from good turns received in the
> past, were suddenly eliminated, society (at least as we know it) would
> break apart.

39. Simmel, *Conflict*, pp. 117–18 (Simmel's italics). On forgiveness, revenge, and reconciliation, see also Arendt, pp. 236–43.

40. Whether it is effective or successful is another matter.

41. For an alternative view of apology that, despite surface commonalities, is clearly at odds with the one presented here, see Goffman, *Relations in
Public*, pp. 113–14. Cf. also two works that follow Goffman's lead: Schlenker
and Darby, "The Use of Apologies," and Schlenker, pp. 154–57. I shall quote
Goffman's terse remarks in their entirety for two reasons: first, so that the

reader may compare the two perspectives and assess their pertinence to my critique in light of the argument I have been trying to develop in this chapter; second, because virtually every subsequent discussion of the topic relies on Goffman's formulation and his assumptions.

> Although accounts have been treated at considerable length in the literature, especially, as suggested, in the legal literature, apologies have not; yet they are quite central. An apology is a gesture through which an individual splits himself into two parts, the part that is guilty of an offense and the part that dissociates itself from the delict and affirms a belief in the offended rule.
>
> In its fullest form, the apology has several elements: expression of embarrassment and chagrin; clarification that one knows what conduct had been expected and sympathizes with the application of negative sanction; verbal rejection, repudiation, and disavowal of the wrong way of behaving along with vilification of the self so behaved; espousal of the right way and an avowal henceforth to pursue that course; performance of penance and the volunteering of restitution. Note that the offender's willingness to initiate and perform his own castigation has certain unapparent values. Were others to do to him what he is willing to do to himself, he might be obliged to feel affronted and to engage in retaliatory action to sustain his moral worth and autonomy. And he can overstate, or overplay the case against himself, thereby giving to the others the task of cutting the self-derogation short—this latter, in turn, being a function that is safer to lodge with the offended since they are not likely to abuse it, whereas he, the offender, might. As suggested, apologies represent a splitting of the self into a blameworthy part and a part that stands back and sympathizes with the blame giving, and, by implication, is worthy of being brought back into the fold. This splitting is but one instance, and often a fairly crude one, of a much more general phenomenon—the tendency for individuals when in the immediate presence of others to reject somehow a self that then is cast off or withdrawn from. In the case of apologies, there is usually an admission that the offense was a serious or real act. This provides a contrast to another type of splitting, one that supports an account, not an apology, in which the actor projects the offensive act as something not to be taken literally, that is, seriously, or after the act claims that he was not acting seriously.

Goffman thus classifies apology as a form of "remedial work" in face-to-face interaction together with accounts, e.g., explanations, excuses, and pretexts.

All of these are taken as "devices" used by offenders "to change the meaning that otherwise might be given to an act, transforming what could be seen as offensive into what can be seen as acceptable" (p. 109). Although Goffman does distinguish apologies from accounts, their function and resemblance are very close to the latter. Moreover, his analytical focus is exclusively upon the offender and not the relationship. For example, apologies are conceptualized as a "set of moves" or interpersonal management ploys used by socially disembodied actors trying to maximize their (questionable) moral credibility and minimize the possibility of being treated as career or habitual deviants. Closer to our pivotal differences, Goffman argues that an apology entails the "splitting" of the self, whereas I underscore the necessity of "attachment" to the offense in response to a call. Finally, my most serious reservation is that *there is no mention whatsoever of what I take to be central to apology: sorrow and regret*. Thus it is conceivable that an actor could follow all the steps described by Goffman without producing a speech act that is socially recognizable as an apology or, its moral reciprocal, forgiveness. All this notwithstanding, Goffman is the only major sociologist to recognize the importance of apology, and his formulations have been indispensable in the honing of my own.

42. *The Anatomy of Dependence*. See also Wagatsuma and Rosett, "The Implications of Apology"; Haley, "Comment"; Benedict, *The Chrysanthemum and the Sword*; and Lebra, *Japanese Patterns of Behavior*. Lebra notes that "even the child on his mother's back is told to bow and say hello to acquaintances she meets on the street. Emphasis is consistently placed on expressing thanks for favors and apology for wrongdoing" (p. 148). I am indebted to Robert J. Smith, Cornell University, for bringing some of these sources to my attention and for sharing his keen insights into Japanese apology through personal correspondence. He is not, of course, responsible for the way in which I have interpreted the materials. According to him, the only person who stands outside the complex hierarchy (which includes the living and the dead) is the emperor.

43. Doi, p. 50.

44. Doi, pp. 50–51.

45. *Winnipeg Free Press*, 26 January 1980. In both civil and criminal cases in Japan, apologies and other signs of repentance are always taken into account and invariably result in lighter sentences for offenders. Courts may also require a public notice of apology, e.g., in newspapers, as part of their judgments in civil suits involving defamation. On these and related points, see Tanaka, pp. 316–30, and Koshi, pp. 17–39. The same holds true, albeit

in a somewhat more restricted way, in North America, as the following examples show. The first is a story by B. J. Delconte, "Give Up, Officials Urge Fugitive," published in the *Winnipeg Sun*, 12 October 1983:

> The person who ran down and killed little Bradley Bluecoat is quickly running out of time.
>
> The hunt for the man is in high gear, and legal experts warn that justice will be especially harsh if he's caught before he comes forward to confess.
>
> They say he'd be doing himself a favor if he willingly tells all immediately.
>
> "It makes all the difference in the world," said Vaughn Baird, QC, a lawyer with 30 years experience.
>
> "If the person has shown no thought or conscience, the courts wonder if they should show him any leniency," he said.
>
> "He must admit he's wrong and show he wants forgiveness," he added.
>
> Chief Justice of the Provincial Court Harold Gyles said that "if an accused has been cooperative with the police, it's generally brought to the court's attention."
>
> "Quite often, it's taken into consideration in sentencing the person," he added.
>
> Crown Attorney Wayne Myshkowsky indicated that a confession is an important first step for the man.
>
> "If he confesses, without being caught first, he's much more likely to get bail," said Myshkowsky.
>
> He said that as far as a court appearance is concerned, "some sentencing authorities say a guilty plea is considered evidence of remorse."
>
> He said that the chance of the court being lenient is increased if remorse is a factor in a case.

Much closer in spirit to the Japanese way of handling such matters, though by no means as widespread, is the procedure described in the news report reproduced on p. 140.

46. Doi, pp. 31–32. Addressing the same issue, Lebra suggests, "Perhaps the *on* [a benefit or benevolence given with a debt or obligation thus incurred] debtor feels at the same time grateful to and sorry for the *on* creditor, either because he is aware of the creditor's sacrifice in his behalf or because he feels incapable of repaying the debt fully. When a Japanese wants to express sincere gratitude, he feels urged to say 'I'm sorry,' since 'thank you'

CRIMINAL'S APOLOGY

Thomas E. Kirby was convicted of Burglary First Degree for burglarizing a residence in South Beach, Oregon on October 25, 1985. He has previously been convicted of burglary in Portland. He was placed on probation to the Corrections Division on March 7, 1986 and ordered to make restitution, pay a fine, perform community service and place this ad in the Newport News-Times apologizing for his conduct. At the time of his arrest, he was in a residence on Sam Creek Road in the Toledo/Newport area. Prior to this he resided in Waldport.

APOLOGY

I, Tom Kirby, wish to apologize to the people of the City of Newport for all of the problems I have caused. I know now what I did was selfish and wrong. I also realize that I have caused a lot of hardships on people that were my friends and also my own family.

I want to thank the courts for a second chance to prove that I can be an honest upstanding person.

My apologies again for causing any inconveniences to anyone.

Tom E. Kirby

CRIME STOPPERS TIP: As the jails and penitentiaries fill up and criminals remain in the community, be aware of which of your neighbors pose a threat to you and your family. Don't hesitate to call a person's probation officer or the police if you observe any suspicious activity on their part. Be aware of who has been convicted of crimes and who may be committing crimes in your neighborhood.

This paid advertisement originally appeared in the Newport, Oregon, *News-Times*. It is reproduced here from the August 1986 issue of *Harper's* magazine, which reported that "under a program established by Lincoln District Attorney Ulys J. Stapleton, people found guilty of crimes against property can take out advertisements apologizing for their crimes instead of serving prison terms."

does not sound sincere enough. This is one of the typical mistakes Japanese make in their interactions with English-speakers, the latter being likely to say, 'Why sorry?'" Lebra, p. 92.

47. Doi, p. 50.

48. Doi, pp. 55–56. As we have seen, this possibility was stressed by Ambrose Bierce.

49. Foucault's interpretation of the historical secularization and redeployment of the sacramental confession, at least in its ideal form, projects this tendency even further and serves to anticipate some of our objections to the notion that Westerners apologize less often than do Japanese. It should be reiterated here that confession, apart from its sacramental nature, is not the same as apology but rather one stage in a process that is closely akin to that of apology. Thus one may confess to something without necessarily being sorry or asking for forgiveness. Hence, the traditional emphasis placed on genuine contrition, an inner conversion, and faith for full absolution and reconciliation.

> Next to testing rituals, next to the testimony of witnesses, and the learned methods of observation and demonstration, the confession became one of the West's most highly valued techniques for producing truth. We have since become a singularly confessing society. The confession has spread its effects far and wide. It plays a part in justice, medicine, education, family relationships, and love relations, in the most ordinary affairs of everyday life, and in the most solemn rites; one confesses one's crimes, one's sins, one's thoughts and desires, one's illnesses and troubles; one goes about telling, with the greatest precision, whatever is most difficult to tell. One confesses in public and in private to one's parents, one's educators, one's doctor, to those one loves; one admits to oneself, in pleasure and in pain, things it would be impossible to tell anyone else, the things people write books about. One confesses— or is forced to confess. When it is not spontaneous or dictated by some internal imperative, the confession is wrung from a person by violence or threat; it is driven from its hiding place in the soul, or extricated from the body. Since the Middle Ages, torture has accompanied it like a shadow, and supported it when it could go no further: the dark twins. The most defenseless tenderness and the bloodiest powers have a similar need to confess. Western man has become a confessing animal. Foucault, p. 59.

50. Doi, p. 52. In personal correspondence, Robert J. Smith writes:

"*Sumanai* or *moshiwake nai* are virtually interchangeable, but the latter is marginally more likely to be used as 'guilt' apology. *Sumanai* may often be correctly translated simply as 'Thank you,' when one is merely acknowledging a favor, while *moshiwake nai* never translates so."

51. "Members generally make a distinction between knowing what they are doing (theoretical action) in the sense that the actor can be said to formulate what he is doing in terms of some rule or criterion; and not knowing what they are doing (practical action), in the sense that the actor is unable to so formulate what he is doing." McHugh, pp. 165–66.

52. Which, of course, is not to argue that a child is incapable of formulating an authentic apology, cannot distinguish between an apology and an excuse, or that a child's apology is ipso facto suspect or invalid. The issue is not age but demonstrated responsibility that coincides with membership.

53. As Hepworth and Turner note with regard to confession, it "was not only important for maintaining orthodox belief, but also for defining appropriate attitudes and character. The final social function of confession . . . is the part confession of sin plays in the definition of what counts as 'human character' in a society. Demonstrations of guilt, remorse, and repentance provide evidence that the penitent, no matter how gross the sin, is also capable of human feeling, capable of responding to the confessor in a manner characteristic of ordinary human beings. Contrition is evidence that a person is worthy of restoration not only to his particular family, but to humanity as such." Hepworth and Turner, pp. 44–45.

54. Although we shall deal with this point more closely in the following chapter, one analyst has carefully documented cases of corporate actions that, if committed by private individuals, would have resulted in criminal trials with possible death sentences. This is hardly news to social and political scientists, historians, journalists, and certainly not to those engaged in corporate law. What concerns us is that not one of those corporated actors ever apologized. Stone, *Where the Law Ends*.

55. *New York Times*, 29 April 1981.

56. *Time*, 19 June 1972.

Chapter 3

1. All the more remarkable, as we have seen, on other grounds as well. Just as the placement of Poe's purloined letter thwarted the most diligent, if unimaginative, investigators, just so is the mysterious regenerative power of an effective apology. Thus it is the *only* solution, short of mutual destruction,

enervating litigation, and social alienation, to certain predicaments, and yet remains unobtrusive and speaks softly.

2. Arendt, p. 237.

3. Cf. Bateson on the primacy of the relationship:

Relationship is always a product of double description.

It is correct (and a great improvement) to begin to think of the two parties to the interaction as two eyes, each giving a monocular view of what goes on and, together, giving a binocular view in depth. This double view *is* the relationship.

Relationship is not internal to the single person. It is nonsense to talk about "dependency" or "aggressiveness" or "pride," and so on. All such words have their roots in what happens between persons, not in some something-or-another inside a person.

No doubt there is a learning in the more particular sense. There are changes in A and changes in B which correspond to the dependency-succorance of the relationship. But the relationship comes first: it *precedes*. Bateson, *Mind and Nature*, pp. 132–33 (Bateson's italics).

4. *A fortiori*, in the case of forgiveness, as captured neatly and sweetly in John Dryden's line, "Forgiveness to the injured doth belong." Cf. George Steiner's convictions that:

Only those who actually passed through hell, who survived Auschwitz after seeing their parents flogged to death or gassed before their own eyes (like Elie Wiesel), or who found their own kin amid the corpses from which they had to extract gold teeth, a daily encounter in Treblinka, can have the right to forgive. *We* do not have that right. This is an important point, often misunderstood. What the Nazis did in the camps and torture chambers is wholly unforgivable, it is a brand on the image of man and will last; each of us has diminished by the enactment of a potential sub-humanity latent in all of us. But if one did not undergo the thing, hate or forgiveness are spiritual games—serious games no doubt—but games none the less. The best now, after so much has been set forth is, perhaps to be silent; not to add to the trivia of literary, sociological debate, to the unspeakable. Steiner, p. 253 (Steiner's italics).

But consider an unusual and dramatic exception to third-party forgiveness:

KINSHASA, Zaire (AP)—Pope John Paul II proclaimed a 25-year-old nun as black Africa's first woman martyr of the Roman Catholic Church yesterday and publicly forgave the soldier who killed her for resisting his rape attempt. . . .

Departing from his prepared text, the Pope referred to Anuarite's convicted killer, former colonel Pierre Openge Olombe, who asked in vain to meet the pontiff to express remorse.

"I myself, in the name of the whole church, forgive (him) with all my heart," John Paul said. "Pope beatifies nun, forgives her murderer," *Winnipeg Free Press*, 16 August 1985.

5. Except, of course, when one or both parties are somehow incapacitated but still able to convey their wishes through another, or when there are language barriers between the principals. In Western societies, the powerful and privileged may delegate their agents or lawyers to do it for them. This practice effectively reduces apology to the status of a legal formality or public relations performance.

6. Religious confession, which in both Western and Eastern Christendom is predicated on an offense, i.e., *sin*, against God (as well as the offended and community), is a special case. On the one hand, the authoritative confessor could be viewed as a mediator, a forgiver by proxy. Nevertheless, since the Middle Ages the role of the priest or confessor has been defined as mandatory and necessary for absolution and reinstatement of the sinner in the spiritual community. In this sense, and because there is no absolution with contrition, the priest effectively serves as the necessary other and *not* as a surrogate. Were he the latter, this would render confession an occasion for self-apology and self-forgiveness.

7. Although there is good reason to believe that they would have apologized anyway, the fact that they had no political stake in the incident apart from maintaining good relations with Israel (and were not accused of being implicated) lent even greater force and drama to the successful gesture.

8. Here, and in what follows, I draw upon Gulliver's distinction between disagreements and disputes, and his useful discussion of the role of third parties in negotiations. As he notes, "To put the disagreement into the public domain is to put it into a different frame of reference and action. There is, in effect, an announcement that there is a disagreement that is not resolvable by normal, dyadic adjustment and is considered in some sense to be serious and therefore requiring special treatment. . . . The term *public* is used here in specific contrast with *private* and *dyadic*. It does not imply that the disagreement, now a potential dispute, invariably becomes a matter of knowledge, interest, and concern to more or less everyone in the community, for the public is often quite limited." Gulliver, p. 76 (Gulliver's italics).

9. Gulliver, pp. 213–14.

10. Which returns us, once again, to Arendt's point that forgiveness releases us from punishment and revenge and seeks to terminate potentially escalating or vicious circles of action. Arendt, p. 241.

11. On the broader structural significance of third parties, see Simmel, "The Triad," as well as Goode, "A Theory of Role Strain"; Goode, "Norm Commitment"; Caplow, *Two Against One*; Gulliver, chap. 7, "Mediators: Triadic Interaction in the Negotiation Process," pp. 209–31; and Bercovitch, *Social Conflicts and Third Parties*.

12. In part because, as Thomas Schelling points out, third parties have "payoff structures" of their own. *The Strategy of Conflict*, p. 44.

13. On the concept of honor, see, for example, Pitt-Rivers, pp. 503–11, as well as Peristiany, *Honour and Shame*; Wyatt-Brown, *Southern Honor*; and Goode, *The Celebration of Heroes*.

14. *The New Columbia Encyclopedia*, 1975, s.v. "Watergate affair."

15. White, p. 350.

16. This was not, as it turned out, his "final public statement." For an extensive and extremely useful analysis of the role of the media and public opinion as third parties during this period, see Lang and Lang, *The Battle for Public Opinion*.

17. White, p. 343.

18. "Nixon calls Watergate break-in 'very stupid thing to do,'" *Winnipeg Free Press*, 6 April 1984.

19. "*Hubris* is a term applied to any kind of behavior in which one treats other people just as one pleases with an arrogant confidence that one will escape paying any penalty for violating their rights and disobeying any law or moral rule accepted by society, whether or not such a law or rule is regarded as resting ultimately on divine sanctions." Dover, p. 34. In what the media dubbed "Operation Candor," Nixon made a brief tour of the South in November 1973 in an attempt to generate public support for his tarnished administration and his own conduct. In one television appearance, he made a statement that would later haunt him and resurrect charges of deviousness, opportunism, and vindictiveness that had plagued him throughout his long and controversial political career. "Answering a question about his personal finances and tax payments, Nixon addressed the nation at large: 'I want to say this to the television audience. . . . People have got to know whether or not their President is a crook. Well, I am not a crook. I have earned everything I have got.' This was an unhappy choice of words. With them the President had undone much that this carefully managed appearance could

have achieved. He later insisted that the remark was no 'spur-of-the-moment statement' but a calculated answer in 'down-to-earth understandable language' to past attacks on his personal integrity." Lang and Lang, p. 119. Thus, as noted earlier, attention was drawn not only to what he allegedly had done but also to what Nixon *was and always had been*, i.e., unscrupulous.

20. And, as mentioned earlier, this was a correct reading, more so after his pardon than his resignation. See, for example, Lang and Lang, pp. 181–235. With regard to apology as documentation, the Langs also observe:

> What many of the most punitive could not forgive was his failure to level with them. At what point a "full confession" could still have earned Nixon enough points to stave off impeachment is a matter for conjecture. Certainly, once the incriminating tapes surfaced, Nixon could no longer convincingly portray himself as a victim entitled to public sympathy. Since his resignation speech showed no contrition, it could hardly diminish the demand for punishment, only mute it temporarily. However, our reading of the data leads us to suspect that Ford's unconditional pardon would have occasioned less of a storm and even gained wide acceptance if it had been accompanied by an admission of guilt. Ford's explanation that he wanted only "to heal the wounds" would have been more credible and the protest against an unconditional pardon as a violation of "equal treatment before the law" would have been less vehement.
>
> Nixon, having failed to "confess," never became the focus of public sympathy (p. 235).

21. Unless otherwise indicated, what follows is culled from reports and commentaries in the *New York Times*. Although a number of investigations by individuals and commissions were conducted to ascertain the circumstances of the overflight, numerous unanswered questions remain because the flight recorder (black box) was never recovered. For some speculative accounts of precisely what happened, see Rohmer, *Massacre 747*; Dallin, *Black Box*; Clubb, *KAL Flight 007*; and Hersh, *The Target Is Destroyed*.

22. *Facts on File*, 43, 9 September 1983, p. 679. As it turned out, the only apologies offered were by the South Koreans. Airline and government officials made public apologies to the families of the victims and to the nation.

23. Thus saying, in effect, that the attack was not the result of accident or error. This version was not, however, adhered to consistently. About a week after Gromyko's statement, Soviet military authorities maintained that their pilots had mistaken the Boeing 747 for an American RC-135 spy plane. According to an investigation by the International Civil Aviation Organization

(a United Nations agency), the jetliner was not on an espionage mission and the crew was unaware that it was off course and being tracked. The report also suggested that the Soviets may have assumed it was a spy plane, not realizing they were confronting a civilian airliner. In perhaps the most exhaustive study to date, Hersh, *The Target Is Destroyed*, reached essentially the same conclusions. He argued that a human error in the programming of the plane's computer led to its intrusion into Soviet air space, that it was not on an intelligence mission for the CIA, and that the Soviets did not knowingly down the airliner, although they did not make adequate attempts to verify its identity. But what really happened remains unclear. Whether or not it was a case of mistaken identity, the Soviets twice refused American efforts to have them formally accept a note demanding compensation for the victims. In August 1989, a U.S. District Court jury awarded $50 million in punitive damages to the families of 137 of the passengers on the grounds of willful misconduct on the part of the crew and Korean Air Lines. The company planned to appeal the verdict.

24. Charles Krauthammer, "On Apologies, Authentic and Otherwise," *Time*, 10 October 1983 (Krauthammer's italics).

25. Jeffrey Simpson, "The missing apology," *Globe and Mail*, 25 April 1984 (italics supplied). Although nine Canadians who had been subjected to experiments by Cameron reached an out-of-court settlement in their suit against the Central Intelligence Agency for the total sum of $750,000 (to be shared) in October 1988, American officials still did not apologize or admit guilt in the matter. A story carried in the *Globe and Mail* of 7 October 1988, "CIA denies guilt shown by damages," reported:

> The settlement of a lawsuit by a group of Canadians who say they were unwitting victims of mind-control experiments financed by the U.S. Central Intelligence Agency is not an admission of guilt by the CIA, the agency's chief spokesman said yesterday.
>
> While refusing to comment directly on the out-of-court settlement in which nine Canadians will share $750,000 (U.S.), spokesman William Devine said in a statement that the CIA's willingness to pay damages in no way "represents a concession of liability on the part of the agency."
>
> He added: "The agency has consistently maintained that its actions were appropriate at the time."

26. In the same sense that members are not only expected to know the norms of the group but to apply them unless prevented from doing so. On this distinction, see McHugh, pp. 165–70.

27. Although my focus is on the child-child-adult triad in the socialization

process, the example can be generalized as long as the triadic structure obtains. Thus adults, families, and other groups can assume these primary roles in the tuition of apology. For an experimental study of how children (K/first, fourth, and seventh graders) independently formulated and judged offenses with respect to responsibility, consequences, motives, apologies, willingness to forgive, punishment, and moral status of the actor based on hypothetical vignettes, see Darby and Schlenker, "Children's Reactions." The investigators found that apologies generally served to reduce negative evaluations and that more elaborate apologies resulted in less blame, more forgiveness, attributions of greater remorse, and less punishment.

28. Apropos of the pedagogy of generosity—an important element in forgiveness—consider Derrida's gloss on Jean Jacques Rousseau's *Emile*:

> Pedagogy cannot help but encounter the problem of imitation. What is example? Should one educate by example or explanation? Should the teacher make an example of himself and not interfere any further, or pile lesson upon exhortation? And is there virtue in being virtuous by imitation? All these questions are asked in the second book of *Emile*.
>
> The problem at first is knowing how to teach generosity or "liberality" to the child. Even before the word and theme of imitation occupy the front of the stage, the problem of the sign is posed. To teach the child true generosity is to make sure that he is not content only to imitate it. What does it mean to imitate generosity? It is to give signs in the place of things, words in the place of sentiments, money in the place of real goods. Therefore the child must be taught not to imitate liberality and this teaching must combat resistance. The child spontaneously wants to guard his goods and put one off the scent [literally, give away the coin]: "Observe that the only things children are set to give are things of which they do not know the value, bits of metal carried in their pockets for which they have no further use. A child would rather give a hundred coins than one cake" [*Emile*, p. 67]. What one gives easily is not signifiers inseparable from signifieds or things, it is the devalued signifiers. The child would not give away money so easily if he knew how to, or could, do something with it. "But get this prodigal giver to distribute what is dear to him, his toys, his sweets, his own lunch, and we shall soon see if you have made him really generous" (*Emile*, pp. 97–99) [p. 67]. Derrida, p. 204.

For a useful discussion of the relationship between actions and moral orientations in socialization, see Goode, *Principles of Sociology*, pp. 68–72.

29. For a thoughtful, moving, and lucid interpretation of this and other aspects of the poem, see Redfield, *Nature and Culture in the Iliad*. Patterns of apologetic discourse between social superiors and subordinates in various contexts clearly merit further investigation. For example, is it generally so, as suggested to me by William J. Goode in private communication, that the higher the rank of the transgressor, the greater the reluctance to apologize, the less likely the person is to apologize, and the more humiliating it is when an apology is given? For an alternative view, at least in regard to ideal behavior, consider the following:

> General rudeness, or the lack of obeisance to etiquette, is much more of a burden to the poor than to the rich, who can usually pay for special treatment and buy their way out of any trouble caused by their own rude behavior. The concept of noblesse oblige is etiquette's demand that the rich not only avoid taking easy advantage of the poor, but that the rich actually treat the poor more considerately than their peers. One of the most heinous crimes known to etiquette is being rude to a subservient person, such as an employee, who is not in the position to respond in kind. Etiquette considers such behavior far more reprehensible than rudeness toward an equal or a superior. Martin and Stent, p. 253.

30. Dostoevsky, pp. 714–15.

31. Although this mot has been attributed to both Gertrude Stein and Benjamin Jowett, I have been unable to establish its source or authorship after consulting several standard reference works. Like most aphorisms whose philosophical premises are muted by brevity, this one may be interpreted in more than one way. For example, it could be taken as a mandate for hubristic behavior or as a profession of pessimism and futility about the possibility of accurate communication between human beings. Adherence to either view, I submit, would not alter the fact that to fashion a life upon these prescriptions, i.e., never apologize, never explain, would effectively demote or banish sorrow and forgiveness from human affairs and transform those who act upon them into either gods or robots. In the same vein, P. G. Wodehouse at least provides us with a testable sociological rationale for total abstention: "It is a good rule in life never to apologize. The right sort of people do not want apologies, and the wrong sort of people take a mean advantage of them."

Chapter 4

1. For a clear discussion of the criteria that distinguish groups, collectivities, and social categories, see Merton, pp. 338–54. For expositional conve-

nience, I shall use the term "collectivity" with reference to obviously diverse social units while keeping in mind the different discursive contexts attending an apology to, say, a family, ethnic group, formal organization, or those who are alike in some way but are not necessarily in social interaction, such as "senior citizens," the homosexual "community," women, or members of a profession. My rationale for so doing is based on my concern to place conceptual emphasis on the "manyness" of the Other as opposed to differences between various Others.

2. Although the focus in what follows is on collective efforts to receive an apology, it should be noted that a collectivity may refuse to accept an apology from a contrite offender (member or non-member) when the transgression is viewed as taxing the limits of forgiveness. This response effectively deprives the offender of absolution or, in the case of a member, reinstatement. Consider an example reported in the press, which, in certain respects, resembles the Speer case cited earlier:

> TOKYO—The U.S. bombardier who dropped an atomic bomb on Nagasaki 40 years ago has offered a public apology to the city, but the offer has been rejected, an official of the city says.
>
> The official said Kermit Beahan, 66, bombardier on the B-29 which dropped the bomb, had offered to visit Nagasaki to apologize when the city marks the 40th anniversary of the bombing Aug. 9. The bomb killed an estimated 70,000 people and devastated the city.
>
> "We understand his sentiments, but there are many atomic bomb victims who are still suffering and who do not wish to meet this man," said the official. *Winnipeg Free Press,* 21 July 1985.

3. The provisional tone of the preceding paragraphs is not intended to serve as an analytical hedge or stylistic evasion. To argue that the Many enjoy certain advantages vis-à-vis the One is not to say that these will necessarily be used. While we cannot here explore fully the intricacies of social mobilization, it is clear that not all collectivities are aware of, able, or willing to exploit their leverage. Witness, for example, the countless indignities and injustices suffered in silence and resignation by various groups and strata throughout history at the hands of powerful and protected individuals. For our purposes, suffice it to say that the extent to which any collectivity can effectively press its claim for an apology (or any claim, for that matter) will depend, among other things, on its size, relative social standing, ethical code, organization, system of normative controls, material and symbolic resources, perceived interests, power, and support from interested parties.

These considerations affect patterns of interaction with individual members or non-members and other collectivities.

4. Schneider's comments on shame, privacy, and publicity are apropos here, although what he calls the "adulteration of the private realm" leads him in a direction somewhat different from mine:

> The sense of shame protects that which is private from public intrusion.... (p. 40)
>
> ... many matters belong to the private realm because their meaning is altered by public display; their very character requires privacy. Making them public does not simply enlarge the circle of participants; it alters the phenomena.... (p. 43)
>
> Anyone who has undergone a life-threatening experience—being stricken with a potentially fatal disease, receiving an anonymous threat of violence—knows how, beyond the first intimate and needy disclosures to a trusted friend, the indescribable mixture of private feelings can truly be shared only with a very few individuals. Beyond this, a false note intrudes: the general character of the public belies the description of the unbearable aloneness of such moments. The portrayal is no longer of that moment when time stood still and the ground beneath gave way. Each of the qualities and experiences described above—terror, a guilty secret, piety, charity, goodness—are compromised and truncated by the admixture of self-consciousness that accompanies their public display (p. 45). Schneider, *Shame, Exposure, and Privacy.*

Since I take publicity as a given wherever the Many are involved, my concern is to isolate and dissect the kind of speech publicity evokes and demands rather than to demonstrate—as Schneider and others do—how a public display violates what is considered intrinsically private. This interest entails delving into the nature of "the general character of the public" insofar as it shapes apologetic discourse. As will become evident, the very self-consciousness that subverts authenticity in one public context may well validate it in another.

5. More recently there is the sensational and complicated case of Salman Rushdie's novel *The Satanic Verses.* As is common knowledge by now, the author, born to a Moslem family in India but educated in England and now a British citizen, was condemned to death by Iran's late Ayatollah Khomeini in February 1989 for alleged blasphemies against Islam in the book. A bounty of $6.2 million was offered by Iranian religious leaders, and Rushdie was forced to go into hiding, where, at this writing, he remains.

There were serious international tensions and consequences, including riots, deaths, threats, banning of literary works, and Iran's breaking of diplomatic relations with the United Kingdom. Of particular interest to us is a public statement by Rushdie given on 18 February 1989:

> As author of *The Satanic Verses*, I recognize that Moslems in many parts of the world are genuinely distressed by the publication of my novel. I profoundly regret the distress that publication has occasioned to sincere followers of Islam. Living as we do in a world of many faiths, this experience has served to remind us that we all must be conscious of the sensibilities of others. *Facts on File*, 49, 24 February 1989, p. 117.

Although this was referred to as an "apology" in various quarters and the media, it was rejected by Khomeini and others on the grounds that it concerned the publication of the book and not its contents, and that it did not indicate sufficient repentance. For a thorough and dispassionate study of the complex issues surrounding this continuing controversy, see Ruthven, *A Satanic Affair*.

6. As we have seen, in certain cases, an apology, in conjunction with other acts, such as payment of a fine or community service, may be accepted as an alternative to imprisonment. Here the apology (clear evidence of remorse) is defined as a crucial component of what may be termed a retributive "package" that is taken into consideration with respect to sentencing or probation. Similarly, apology, restitution, and forgiveness play an increasingly important role in American jurisdictions—over forty cities or counties in twenty states in 1986 had Victim Offender Reconciliation Programs. Haley, p. 505.

7. *Winnipeg Free Press*, 5 November 1979.

8. *Winnipeg Free Press*, 10 December 1979.

9. This term is borrowed from Goffman, *Frame Analysis*, p. 15.

10. Reported by Gerald Eskanazi, *New York Times*, 15 May 1975.

11. On the sociology of demotion, see the classic statement by Garfinkel, pp. 420–24.

12. "Total" identities "refer to persons as 'motivational' types rather than as 'behavioral' types, not to what a person may be expected to have done or not to do . . . but to what the group holds to be the ultimate 'grounds' or 'reasons' for his performance." Garfinkel, p. 420.

13. In what follows, of course, we are not concerned with judging Grant or the Mets. As the American "national pastime," baseball has always been sensitive to any whiff of scandal, on or off the playing field. The lifetime ban of Pete Rose in 1989 is a recent case in point. Our primary interest is in how the Jones incident sheds light on our topic.

14. The contrasting responses to revelations of the extra-marital activities of all-star third baseman Wade Boggs of the Boston Red Sox during road trips and other occasions in the late 1980s are instructive with regard to changing mores in the world of sport.

15. Garfinkel, p. 422.

16. Ibid., p. 423.

17. Garfinkel's analysis does not specify or distinguish the membership status of witnesses.

18. Roger Angell, personal communication.

19. *Winnipeg Tribune*, 26 September 1978.

20. The analytical distinction between a disagreement, which essentially entails a dyadic adjustment between the parties themselves, and a dispute is taken from Gulliver, pp. 75–76. To wit: "A dispute becomes imminent only when the two parties are unable and/or unwilling to resolve their disagreement; that is, when one or both are not prepared to accept the status quo (should that any longer be a possibility) or to accede to the demand or denial of demand by the other. A dispute is precipitated by a crisis in the relationship. That crisis comes from the realization by at least one party that dyadic adjustment is unsatisfactory or impossible and that the continued disagreement cannot be tolerated. That person therefore attempts to take the disagreement out of the private, dyadic context and to put it into a public domain with the intent that 'something must be done.' Going into a public domain offers the possibility of appealing to other people and to the interests and norms of the community, which, it is thought, may be advantageous to, and supportive of, the party's demands. Sometimes going public is an attempt to avoid further deterioration of the relationship and of the situation, including a threat of violence or some other unpleasant result."

21. On expected durations and other sociocultural aspects of time, see Zerubavel, *Hidden Rhythms*; Hall, *The Dance of Life*; and Young, *The Metronomic Society*.

22. Judgments, by the way, that others may make but that effectively rest with the principals when all is said and done.

23. Ishiguro, p. 155.

24. As chillingly depicted in Kafka's *The Trial* or one of its worthy descendants, Bernard Malamud's *The Fixer*.

25. A notable and notorious example of one such extreme is the case of the English traitor and spy Anthony Blunt, as described in an essay by George Steiner:

It is Blunt's condescension, the intact carapace of his self-esteem which struck those who have sought him out since his public exposure. Hardened souls in journalism have recoiled from the man's cold sophistries, from the edge of self-satisfaction with which he savoured the smoked-trout sandwiches thoughtfully put before him by a team of interviewers in the editorial sanctum of the *London Times*. He has depicted his long years of service to the Soviet intelligence organs as marginal, almost amateurish in their significance. He has denied handing over information of any real importance. His implication in the Philby-Burgess-Maclean murk was only that of personal amity, of the decent thing done among kindred souls. His television performance in the third week of November 1979 was a classic. It identified not only the tawdriness of Blunt but, even more disturbingly, that of the medium itself. Here was, as one newspaper later put it, "a man with an infinite capacity for duplicity" doing a silvery, suave little pas de deux before millions. The fine hands wove arabesques suggesting cordial complicities with inquisitors and with a great public that Blunt, fairly enough, must have read as eager and prurient. The mouth moved primly, dropping seemingly hesitant yet elegantly veneered sentences in a minor key characteristic of the Cambridge common rooms of an earlier vintage. *But Professor Blunt's eyes remained as flat and chill as glass.* It was his younger companion, harried by the press and the vileness of it all, who jumped or fell from the window of Blunt's apartment. Blunt himself, seen in Rome in mid-September, was rumoured to be working on his memoirs and apologia in sunny refuge. Steiner, p. 201 (italics supplied).

26. *Winnipeg Free Press*, 13 August 1982 (italics supplied).

27. Alice Krueger, "Food store hard to pin down," *Winnipeg Free Press*, 24 September 1979.

28. Wagatsuma and Rosett, pp. 487–88 (authors' italics).

29. Consider the following account that appeared in the *New York Times* on 4 October 1981 under the headline "War Hero Seized as Deserter."

GRAPEVINE, Tex., Oct. 3 (UPI)—For almost seven years Roque Vela gave his best to the United States Army. He fought in one of Vietnam's most difficult battle zones until a hand grenade knocked him out of the war.

Thirteen years later he endured the humiliation of being hauled out of a birthday party by the Military Police, spread-eagled against a patrol car and searched in front of his friends, and of being held four days while the Army sorted through a bureaucratic blunder.

The Army thought Mr. Vela was a deserter, ignoring his protests and offer to show proof of his honorable discharge.

"I was in hell for 10 months in Vietnam as a platoon sergeant in the Mekong Delta, one of the nastiest theaters of the war," said Mr. Vela, who joined the Army in June 1961 and was discharged in January 1968. "I didn't have to go, but I felt it was my duty after all the years that they had trained me. Now it makes me feel heartsick because I have always felt it was an honor to serve in the Army, the same Army that could do this thing."

In a stop at Dallas-Fort Worth Airport Wednesday, while returning to his home in Laredo, Tex., from a military jail at Fort Sill, Okla., the 37-year-old former infantryman told his story.

Last Saturday, while he was at a birthday party, Military Police arrived with a warrant for his arrest. After trying to convince them that it was a mistake and that his honorable discharge was at home, Mr. Vela was searched, while his friends watched in shock, and driven to the Webb County Jail. He repeatedly asked the Military Police to get in touch with the provost marshall's office at Fort Sam Houston in San Antonio where his record could be verified.

But Mr. Vela was held in jail, having been informed that he had been considered absent without leave since July 15, 1967.

He was released Tuesday after a lawyer, Joe Rubio, hired retired Sgt. Maj. Luis Ladin to cut through the red tape and find the problem.

The Pentagon file on Mr. Vela had not been kept up to date and a field file was burned with thousands of others in a 1973 fire at a St. Louis records center.

Mr. Vela was awarded the Army Commendation Medal for Valor for organizing his troops under fire in an ambush in Vietnam. He was wounded by hand grenade fragments in early 1967 and was awarded a Purple Heart.

Senator John Tower of Texas, chairman of the Senate Armed Services Committee, apologized yesterday to Mr. Vela, saying: "On behalf of all Americans who appreciate your valorous service in Vietnam, I wish to extend my apologies."

30. For an extremely useful discussion of the sociohistorical development of modern "juristic persons" or corporate actors and their relations with "natural persons," see Coleman, *Power and the Structure of Society*.

31. Which is *not* to argue that collectivities or institutions do not play a critical role in shaping the ways individuals perceive, think, and feel about their social worlds. On these and related points about the nature of suprapersonal corporate bodies, see Douglas, *How Institutions Think*.

32. Needless to say, the qualification "for the most part" is called for in light of the considerable sums of money spent by corporate actors (private and public) on advertising designed to depict themselves as natural persons with positive human faculties and symbolic associations, e.g., caring, friendly, and so on.

33. To argue that corporate actors cannot fully reproduce the moral faculties of human agents or natural persons is not to discount their capabilities for acting "humanely" in their dealings with the latter. In this regard, as Wagatsuma and Rosett remind us, standard Japanese practices are instructive.

34. Just as the absence of an apology to Mrs. Houliston from Safeway contributed to her distress. On the other hand, Mr. Vela's reaction to Senator Tower's apology "on behalf of all Americans" and, presumably, the United States Army remains unknown.

35. Of course, this is not to imply that interpersonal apology takes place in a social vacuum or is merely the business of the offending and offended parties. The contrast, rather, has to do with the extent to which responsibility for transgression is seen as resting with individuals or in their capacities as group members.

36. The phrase in quotation marks is borrowed from Bourdieu, p. 21.

37. What is off the record may come to be placed on record in a variety of ways we cannot pursue here. But until this happens, it exists in a discursive domain devoid of collective responsibility or moral obligation. The distinction between "on record" and "off the record" discourse draws heavily upon Bourdieu's discussion of what he calls "officializing strategies." Bourdieu, pp. 38–43.

38. These functions may also be performed by outsiders, as exemplified by the work of such organizations as Amnesty International.

39. This also means, as we shall see, that such matters as when the transgression occurred, the presence or absence of those directly involved, or how the apology came to be put on record are secondary. To repeat: the record comes first.

40. The distinction we are drawing between collective and personal linguistic codes in apologetic discourse corresponds, albeit in a more restricted fashion, to what Bourdieu and Passeron formulate as "bourgeois parlance and common parlance" in their study of French higher education. Bourdieu and Passeron, pp. 114–30. Needless to say, individuals are not necessarily immune to institutionally fashioned speech in their personal relations. But when it comes to apology and other speech acts, this detached style, unless

intentionally ironic or playful, is dissonant. It is inappropriate and adulterating because it distances the offender from the transgression and the offended party.

41. I am here referring to the apology itself, even when extensive and detailed accounts of wrongs have been gathered and officially recorded by victims, the offenders themselves, or interested third parties.

42. For a useful analysis of such linguistic displacements, see Ong, *Orality and Literacy*. It should also be noted that the collective record and memory are subject to periodic and selective reinterpretation. See, as a case in point, Fitzgerald, *America Revised*.

43. I have not included the previously discussed Lod Airport or Korean Air Lines Flight 007 incidents. All the examples cited are from journalistic sources.

44. A record, by the way, to which other groups with similar grievances can refer as precedent in pressing their own claims.

45. "Healing the wounds: Church's apology to Indians renews pride in congregations," reported by Doreen Martens in the *Winnipeg Free Press*, 5 September 1987. This lengthy piece recapitulates the earlier story and provides further elucidation on the incident and its immediate consequences.

46. John Allemang, "Regret, joy mark formation of church body for natives," *Globe and Mail*, 18 August 1988.

47. In general, the same holds for interpersonal apology: a self-initiated admission of wrongdoing and sorrow gives the offender a moral edge and presses the victim to respond one way or another. At the same time, there is greater discursive flexibility in this form than in collective interaction.

48. Although it is difficult to ascertain whether the two events were connected, at the same meeting where native members responded to the apology they had received, the general council of the church decided against formally apologizing to Jews for ignoring the Holocaust. An excerpt from an account by David Roberts in the *Winnipeg Free Press* of 24 August 1988 entitled, "United Church decides against apology to Jews," informs us:

> Myrna Livingstone . . . , a commissioner to the council and member of a special committee that drafted the recommendations, said the panel was ready to ask the church to apologize to Jews until members spoke to a Toronto rabbi, Jordan Pearlson.
>
> "He said that following so closely on the heels of the last apology (made by the church to native Canadians in 1986) that an apology would lose some of its meaning," Livingstone said yesterday.

However, she said the church hasn't ruled out a future apology after consultation with the Jewish community.

Sociologically, the church's apparent penchant for apologizing—witness the Reverend Endicott example discussed earlier—could be seen as the institutional counterpart of chronic and compulsive individual apology. Moreover, as the above report indicates, a law of diminishing marginal utility is at work in the economy of apology. Needless to say, both phenomena would color collective perceptions and reactions to repeated apology by the Many and merit further investigation.

Chapter 5

1. For example, "To the extent that these three criteria—enduring and morally established forms of social interaction, self-definition as a member and the same definition by others—are fully met, those involved in the sustained interaction are clearly identifiable as comprising groups." Merton, p. 340.

2. Peli, pp. 91–92. These comments on the revelatory power of the spoken word echo those of Ong and Arendt cited earlier, but with a somewhat different resonance.

3. I am indebted to Hubert J. O'Gorman for bringing this issue to my attention. A case in point is the following account that appeared under the headline, "Party leader assails group over apology," in the *Globe and Mail* of 28 May 1990:

> A delegation from nearby Brockville should not have apologized for an incident in which people wiped their feet on the Quebec flag, the leader of a pro-English fringe party said on Saturday.
>
> "How many times has the Canadian flag been publicly burned in Quebec and have the Quebec people sent delegates to apologize for that—no way," said Gordon McGregor, leader of the Ontario arm of the Confederation of Regions party, which held its national convention in this St. Lawrence River town about 50 kilometres east of Brockville, on the weekend.
>
> A delegation of clergy and politicians went to Montreal last Thursday to apologize for the incident last September during which about a half-dozen members of another anti-bilingualism group—the Alliance for the Preservation of English in Canada—stomped on the Quebec flag.
>
> The apology was the latest example of Canada bowing to Quebec,

Mr. McGregor said in an interview during the convention, which drew about 400 delegates.

The party based in Edmonton was founded about five years ago to promote Western separation but has since switched its emphasis to language.

It wants English as the only official language in Canada.

4. Although Hepworth and Turner provide a useful overview and analysis of auricular (private) confession, their explicit commitment to Goffman's formulation leads them in directions other than those suggested in this study and hence in the way we would proceed. For example, "Rehabilitation may be a painful process and to regain acceptance it is usually necessary to apologise for the disruption which the deviant act has caused, and even more important, disown the deviant self. Confessions are thus a neglected form of apology which involves the individual separating himself into two parts: the part that is technically guilty of the offence and the part that disowns itself from guilt and swears allegiance to the norms that have been violated." Hepworth and Turner, p. 159. On the institutional development and subjective experience of confession, see also Tentler, *Sin and Confession*.

BIBLIOGRAPHY

Arendt, Hannah. *The Human Condition*. Chicago: University of Chicago Press, 1958.

Austin, John L. *How to Do Things with Words*. Oxford: Oxford University Press, 1962.

———. "A Plea for Excuses." In *Philosophical Papers*. Oxford: Oxford University Press, 1970. 2d ed.

Bateson, Gregory. *Steps to an Ecology of Mind*. New York: Ballantine Books, 1972.

———. *Mind and Nature: A Necessary Unity*. New York: E. P. Dutton, 1979.

Benedict, Ruth. *The Chrysanthemum and the Sword: Patterns of Japanese Culture*. Boston: Houghton Mifflin, 1946.

Bercovitch, Jacob. *Social Conflicts and Third Parties: Strategies of Conflict Resolution*. Boulder, Colo.: Westview Press, 1984.

Bierce, Ambrose. *The Devil's Dictionary*. New York: Dover Press, 1958.

Blau, Peter M. *Exchange and Power in Social Life*. New York: John Wiley, 1964.

Blum-Kulka, Shoshana, Juliane House, and Gabriele Kasper, eds. *Cross-Cultural Pragmatics: Requests and Apologies*. Norwood, N.J.: Ablex, 1989.

Bourdieu, Pierre. *Outline of a Theory of Practice*. Trans. Richard Nice. Cambridge: Cambridge University Press, 1977.

———, and Jean-Claude Passeron. *Reproduction: In Education, Society and Culture*. Trans. Richard Nice. London: Sage Publications, 1977.

Campbell, J. K. *Honour, Family and Patronage: A Study of Institutions and Moral Values in a Greek Mountain Community*. Oxford: Clarendon Press, 1964.

Caplow, Theodore. *Two Against One: Coalitions in Triads*. Englewood Cliffs, N.J.: Prentice-Hall, 1968.

Clubb, Oliver. *KAL Flight 007: The Hidden Story*. Sag Harbor, N.Y.: The Permanent Press, 1985.

Coleman, James S. *Power and the Structure of Society*. New York: W. W. Norton, 1974.

Coulmas, Florian. "'Poison to Your Soul' Thanks and Apologies Contrastively Viewed." In *Conversational Routine*, ed. Florian Coulmas, 69–91. The Hague: Mouton, 1981.

Dallin, Alexander. *Black Box: KAL 007 and the Superpowers*. Berkeley: University of California Press, 1985.

Darby, Bruce W., and Barry R. Schlenker. "Children's Reactions to Apologies." *Journal of Personality and Social Psychology*, 43 no. 4 (1982), 742–53.

Derrida, Jacques. *Of Grammatology*. Trans. Gayatri C. Spivak. Baltimore: The Johns Hopkins University Press, 1976.

Doi, Takeo. *The Anatomy of Dependence*. Trans. John Bester. New York: Kodansha International, 1973.

Dostoevsky, Fyodor. *The Brothers Karamazov*. Trans. Andrew H. MacAndrew. New York: Bantam Books, 1981.

Douglas, Mary. *How Institutions Think*. Syracuse, N.Y.: Syracuse University Press, 1986.

Dover, Kenneth J. *Greek Homosexuality*. Cambridge, Mass.: Harvard University Press, 1978.

Edmondson, Willis J. "On Saying You're Sorry." In *Conversational Routine*, ed. Florian Coulmas, 274–88. The Hague: Mouton, 1981.

Elias, Norbert. *The Civilizing Process*. Trans. Edmund Jephcott. New York: Urizen Books, 1978.

Fitzgerald, Frances. *America Revised: History Schoolbooks in the Twentieth Century*. New York: Vintage Books, 1979.

Foucault, Michel. *The History of Sexuality*. Trans. Robert Hurley. New York: Vintage Books, 1980.

Fraser, Bruce. "On Apologizing." In *Conversational Routine*, ed. Florian Coulmas, 259–71. The Hague: Mouton, 1981.

Garfinkel, Harold. "Conditions of Successful Degradation Ceremonies." *American Journal of Sociology*, 61 (March 1956), 420–24.

Gennep, Arnold van. *The Rites of Passage*. Trans. Monika V. Vizedom and Gabriella L. Caffee. Chicago: University of Chicago Press, 1960.

Gerbner, George. "Teacher Image and the Hidden Curriculum." *The American Scholar* (Winter 1972–73), 66–92.

Goffman, Erving. *Relations in Public: Microstudies of the Public Order*. New York: Basic Books, 1971.

———. *Frame Analysis: An Essay on the Organization of Experience*. New York: Harper Colophon Books, 1974.

Goode, William J. "A Theory of Role Strain." *American Sociological Review*, 25 (Aug. 1960), 483–96.

———. "Norm Commitment and Conformity to Role-Status Obligations." *American Journal of Sociology*, 66 (Nov. 1960), 246–58.

———. *Principles of Sociology*. New York: McGraw-Hill, 1977.

———. *The Celebration of Heroes: Prestige as a Control System*. Berkeley: University of California Press, 1978.

Gulliver, P. H. *Disputes and Negotiations: A Cross-Cultural Perspective*. New York: Academic Press, 1979.

Haley, John O. "Comment: The Implications of Apology." *Law & Society Review*, 20, no. 4 (1986), 499–507.

Hall, Edward T. *The Dance of Life: The Other Dimension of Time*. New York: Anchor Press/Doubleday, 1983.

Hepworth, Mike, and Bryan S. Turner. *Confession: Studies in Deviance and Religion*. London: Routledge & Kegan Paul, 1982.

Hersh, Seymour. *The Target Is Destroyed*. New York: Random House, 1986.

Hewitt, John P., and Randall Stokes. "Disclaimers." *American Sociological Review*, 40 (Feb. 1975), 1–11.

Homans, George C. *Social Behavior: Its Elementary Forms*. New York: Harcourt Brace & World, 1961.

Ishiguro, Kazuo. *An Artist of the Floating World*. New York: G. P. Putnam's Sons, 1986.

Koshi, George M. *The Japanese Legal Advisor: Crime and Punishments*. Rutland, Vt. and Tokyo: Charles E. Tuttle, 1970.

Kundera, Milan. *The Book of Laughter and Forgetting*. Trans. Michael Henry Heim. New York: Penguin Books, 1981.

Lang, Gladys Engel, and Kurt Lang. *The Battle for Public Opinion: The President, the Press, and the Polls During Watergate*. New York: Columbia University Press, 1983.

Lapham, Lewis H. *Fortune's Child: A Portrait of the United States as Spendthrift Heir*. Garden City, N.Y.: Doubleday, 1980.

Lebra, Takie S. *Japanese Patterns of Behavior*. Honolulu: University of Hawaii Press, 1976.

Malamud, Bernard. *The Fixer*. London: Eyre & Spottiswoode, 1967.

Martin, Judith. *Miss Manners' Guide to Excruciatingly Correct Behavior*. New York: Atheneum, 1982.

———, and Gunther S. Stent. "I Think; Therefore I Thank: A Philosophy of Etiquette." *The American Scholar* (Spring 1990), 237–54.

McHugh, Peter. "A Common-Sense Perception of Deviance." In *Recent Sociology No. 2: Patterns of Communicative Behaviour*, ed. Hans P. Dreitzel, 152–80. New York: Macmillan, 1970.

Merton, Robert K. *Social Theory and Social Structure*. Enlarged ed. New York: The Free Press, 1968.

Nagano, Miho. " 'How to Say I'm Sorry': The Use of Apologies in Japan and the United States." Master's thesis, San Francisco State University, 1985.

Nicolson, Harold. *Good Behaviour: Being a Study of Certain Types of Civility*. Boston: Beacon Press, 1960.

Ong, Walter J. *The Presence of the Word*. New York: Simon & Schuster, 1970.

———. *Interfaces of the Word: Studies in the Evolution of Consciousness and Culture*. Ithaca, N.Y.: Cornell University Press, 1977.

———. *Orality and Literacy: The Technologizing of the Word*. New York and London: Methuen, 1982.

Partridge, Eric. *Origins: A Short Etymological Dictionary of Modern English*. New York: Macmillan, 1977.

Peli, Pinchas H. *Soloveitchik on Repentance: The Thought and Oral Discourses of Rabbi Joseph B. Soloveitchik*. New York: Paulist Press, 1984.

Peristiany, J. G., ed. *Honour and Shame: The Values of Mediterranean Society*. Chicago: University of Chicago Press, 1966.

Pitt-Rivers, Julian. "Honor." In *International Encyclopedia of the Social Sciences*, ed. David L. Sills. New York: Macmillan, 1968, 6:503–11.

Post, Elizabeth L. *The New Emily Post's Etiquette*. New York: Funk and Wagnalls, 1975.

Redfield, James M. *Nature and Culture in the Iliad: The Tragedy of Hector*. Chicago: University of Chicago Press, 1975.

Rohmer, Richard. *Massacre 747: The Story of Korean Air Lines Flight 007*. Markham, Ontario: PaperJacks, 1984.

Ruthven, Malise. *A Satanic Affair: Salman Rushdie and the Rage of Islam*. New York: Random House, 1990.

Scheler, Max. "Repentance and Rebirth." In *On the Eternal in Man*, 35–65. Trans. Bernard Noble. London: SCM Press, 1960.

Schelling, Thomas C. *The Strategy of Conflict*. Cambridge, Mass.: Harvard University Press, 1960.

Schlenker, Barry R. *Impression Management*. Monterey, Calif.: Brooks/Cole, 1980.

————, and Bruce W. Darby. "The Use of Apologies in Social Predicaments." *Social Psychology Quarterly*, 44 (Sept. 1981), 271–78.

Schneider, Carl D. *Shame, Exposure, and Privacy*. Boston: Beacon Press, 1977.

Scott, Marvin B., and Stanford M. Lyman. "Accounts." *American Sociological Review*, 33 (Feb. 1968), 46–62.

Searle, John R. *Speech Acts: An Essay in the Philosophy of Language*. Cambridge: Cambridge University Press, 1969.

Semin, G. R., and A. S. R. Manstead. *The Accountability of Behavior: A Social Psychological Analysis*. New York: Academic Press, 1983.

Simmel, Georg. "Faithfulness and Gratitude." In *The Sociology of Georg Simmel*. Ed. and trans. Kurt H. Wolff. Glencoe, Ill.: The Free Press, 1950.

————. "The Triad." In *The Sociology of Georg Simmel*, 145–69.

————. *Conflict*. Trans. Kurt H. Wolff. Glencoe, Ill.: The Free Press, 1955.

Snyder, C. R., Raymond L. Higgens, and Rita J. Stucky. *Excuses: Masquerades in Search of Grace*. New York: John Wiley, 1983.

Steiner, George. *George Steiner: A Reader*. New York: Oxford University Press, 1984.

Stone, Christopher. *Where the Law Ends: Social Control of Corporate Behavior*. New York: Harper & Row, 1975.

Tanaka, Hideo, ed. *The Japanese Legal System: Introductory Cases and Materials*. Tokyo: University of Tokyo Press, 1976.

Tentler, Thomas N. *Sin and Confession on the Eve of the Reformation*. Princeton: Princeton University Press, 1977.

Turner, Victor W. *The Ritual Process: Structure and Anti-Structure*. Chicago: Aldine, 1969.

Vanderbilt, Amy. *The Amy Vanderbilt Complete Book of Etiquette: A Guide to Contemporary Living*. Revised and expanded by Letitia Baldridge. New York: Doubleday, 1978.

Wagatsuma, Hiroshi, and Arthur Rosett. "The Implications of Apology: Law and Culture in Japan and the United States." *Law & Society Review*, 20, no. 4 (1986), 461–98.

White, Theodore H. *Breach of Faith: The Fall of Richard Nixon*. New York: Atheneum, 1975.

Wyatt-Brown, Bertram. *Southern Honor: Ethics and Behavior in the Old South*. New York: Oxford University Press, 1982.

Young, Michael. *The Metronomic Society: Natural Rhythms and Human Timetables*. Cambridge, Mass.: Harvard University Press, 1988.

Zerubavel, Eviatar. *Hidden Rhythms: Schedules and Calendars in Social Life*. Chicago: University of Chicago Press, 1981.

Library of Congress Cataloging-in-Publication Data

Tavuchis, Nicholas, 1934–
    Mea culpa: a sociology of apology and reconciliation / Nicholas
Tavuchis.
        p.   cm.
    Includes bibliographical references.
    ISBN 0-8047-1936-5 (alk. paper):
    1. Apologizing.   2. Reconciliation.   1. Title.
BF575.A75T38   1991
302'.1—dc20
91-16463
CIP

∞   This book has been typeset in 10/13 Galliard by Tseng Information
Systems, Inc. It is printed on acid-free paper.